HOW RELIABLE IS NATIONAL CURRICULUM ASSESSMENT?

Edited by
Dougal Hutchison
Ian Schagen

Published in April 1994
by the National Foundation for Educational Research,
The Mere, Upton Park, Slough, Berkshire SL1 2DQ

Registered Charity No. 313392
ISBN 0 7005 1359 0

CONTENTS

INTRODUCTION

Before the National Curriculum came on the scene and the methods for assessing it were proposed, the concepts of validity and reliability were widely used and understood in terms of the standardised, multi-item, norm-referenced tests in common use. Statistics called 'reliability measures' or just 'reliabilities' were routinely calculated and were assumed to have clear and direct relevance to the evaluation of such tests and their use in assessing pupils. Some authors (see for example, Loevinger, 1947) had cast doubt on these usages, but in general most problems of measuring reliability were assumed to be solved.

Then a new day dawned in England and Wales, and a National Curriculum was introduced, together with requirements for assessment which were radically different from the tests currently in use. National Curriculum Assessment (NCA) was to be criterion-referenced; it would be based on both teacher assessment (TA) as well as standard assessment tasks (SATs); it would assess children on a ten-level scale which would be consistent across subjects and subject areas; and it would make use of assessments which were directly relevant to classroom experience rather than conventional paper and pencil tests.

Time has told and will tell how many of these expectations came or will come to pass, and how many were and will be modified in practice, as reality and political pressure have had their way with the initial utopian dreams. But a radical difference still remains between NCA and conventional norm-referenced tests. Fuller details of the National Curriculum, and the development of its assessment, are given in Chapter 1.

It is probably true that the original begetters of NCA paid little attention to the question of measuring validity and reliability because they assumed that these properties would flow naturally from the criterion-referenced design of the assessment. The Task Group on Assessment and Testing (TGAT) in their report (DES/Welsh Office, 1987) devoted a two-page appendix to reliability, validity and error, but this confined itself to generalities and said little that was practical concerning the measurement of these quantities, apart from recommending generalisability theory as an approach. Unfortunately, this guidance has failed to lead to any usable method for measuring the reliability of NCA.

The development of NCA proceeded apace, starting with the youngest age group, and the production of assessments has largely kept well ahead of theoretical research into their validity and reliability. Only when the time came to evaluate the results of the innovative assessments were questions raised as to the reliability of the outcomes, in the broad sense, and the poverty of our theoretical base was then laid bare. The aim of this book is to summarise the attempts which have been made to 'catch up' with NCA and develop theoretical and practical tools for evaluating the assessment methods and outcomes.

In September 1993 a symposium was held as part of the British Educational Research Association conference at Liverpool University, with the purpose of bringing together researchers in this general area to discuss the issues and possible ways forward. Six papers were presented, all of which are printed in this book. Valuable insights were gained from the views of discussants, two of whom contributed expanded notes for this book. It is hoped that the symposium and this compilation will inspire researchers to develop new theoretical frameworks and practical methods for evaluating NCA reliability and validity, which are widely applicable not just to the present structures and modes of assessment, but to the forms they may assume in the future.

The symposium was chaired by Ray Sumner, Head of the Department of Information and External Services at the National Foundation for Educational Research (NFER). Dr Sumner has a wide range of experience of the use of assessment results to inform schools, parents and other interested parties, and his introductory remarks aim to set the symposium papers into the context of the ever-changing political and educational scene.

As an introduction to the symposium papers, the first chapter has been contributed by Marian Sainsbury, leader of the team largely responsible for developing the innovative Key Stage 1 standard assessments. This is entitled 'The Structure of National Curriculum Assessment', and gives an overview of the subject, setting in context the later papers and showing how the methods of assessment have changed and developed under political and practical pressures.

Chapter 2 has been written by Dylan Wiliam, of King's College London, with the title 'Reconceptualising Validity, Dependability and Reliability for National Curriculum Assessment'. His experience in working for the CATS team developing Key Stage 3 assessments has given him excellent credentials for this work, and the first part consists of a valuable summary of the many different ways in which validity has been defined. He then proceeds to examine concepts of reliability and dependability, and concludes that signal detection theory is a useful way of looking at the problem of setting the 'mastery' threshold for criterion-referenced systems such as NCA.

Chapter 3, 'The Reliability of National Curriculum Assessment at Key Stages 1 and 2', has been contributed by Diane Shorrocks and Nick Nelson, members of a team at Leeds University which has been evaluating the assessments developed by other centres, as well as recently developing assessment materials themselves for mathematics at Key Stage 2. The main thrust of the evaluation was to compare the levels assigned to pupils by the teacher assessment and the standard tasks, and also by special in-depth instruments of their own. The results of these comparisons are interesting, and have much to say about the reliability of NCA. The authors go on to discuss issues concerning the proper allocation of test items to curriculum domains, given constraints on the overall 'manageability' of the assessment.

Ann Filer, a research student at West of England University, has written Chapter 4, 'Teacher Assessment: A Sociological Perspective', based on her detailed investigation of classroom practices as she followed a cohort of pupils through Years 1, 2 and 3 of the National Curriculum. This chapter shows how teacher strategies can create a context which favours certain pupils at the expense of others, and gives examples of how this occurs. The sociological perspective gives different insights into the problems of NCA reliability from those obtained via more technological, statistical analyses.

Alastair Pollitt of the University of Cambridge has contributed Chapter 5, 'Measuring and Evaluating Reliability in National Curriculum Assessment'. The crux of his argument is that 'reliability', as conventionally defined and measured, is not useful for NCA and it is more revealing to estimate standard errors and misclassification probabilities. Problems inherent in the NCA system are pointed out, in particular the difficulty that the assessments are meant to fulfil many different and incompatible functions. Finally, the author points out that the most serious error that can occur is not unreliability, but bias, which is perpetuated unchanged into aggregated results, such as the ubiquitous 'league tables'.

Chapter 6, 'Graphical Representation of the Reliability of National Curriculum Assessment', has been written by Ian Schagen, a statistician at the NFER who has been heavily involved in the analysis of the early Key Stage 1 assessments, as well as the evaluation of Key Stage 3 tests. His procedure is to fit a simple model of item difficulties and pupil potential attainment to NCA data, and then use the model, in combination with the aggregation rules in force for the particular attainment target, to estimate the variance in the assigned level as a function of pupil potential attainment. Plotted as a graph, this gives useful insights into the way an assessment is working and its possible deviations from the optimal pattern. Examples of such graphs are given, and simulations are used to validate the results.

Dougal Hutchison, Chief Statistician at the NFER, is the author of Chapter 7, 'Modelling Adaptive Assessment at Key Stage 1'. One of the major innovations at Key Stage 1 has been the introduction of adaptive tests, in which each pupil is only tested at relevant levels. This opens up questions about the extent to which the adaptive tests are as reliable as equivalent assessments in which all items are covered, and the amount of time or effort saved by the modification. Through the use of IRT-based models and extensive simulations, the author has answered these questions and points the way to the use of such methods in other types of detailed analysis of the outcomes of NCA.

Chapter 8 consists of the reactions of eminent discussants to the material presented at the symposium and collected in this volume. Caroline Gipps, of the University of London Institute of Education, is President of BERA and a member of its Policy Task Group on Assessment. Rob Taylor was a member of the Evaluation and Monitoring Unit at the School Examinations and Assessment Council (SEAC), and has long had a keen interest in issues of reliability and validity, particularly from a policy-maker's perspective. Tom Christie, of the Centre for Formative Assessment Studies at the Universaity of Manchester, has a wide knowledge of the development and evolution of National Curriculum Assessment. Together the discussants are able to put the whole set of issues addressed in this volume into context, and to point out ways in which future developments, both theoretical and practical, could lead to worthwhile advances in understanding for all involved in the process of National Curriculum Assessment.

The views expressed in the following chapters are those of the contributing authors and are not necessarily the views of the National Foundation for Educational Research.

The editors wish to express their thanks to all those involved in the seminar and the subsequent production of this book, including the chairman, contributors and discussants. Especial mention should be made of Christine Webster, who handled most of the administration and prepared much of the book for publication, in collaboration with Mary Hargreaves. Thanks are also due to David Upton for editing the manuscripts, to Tim Wright for designing the cover, and to Enver Carim for overseeing the production and publication.

References

DES/WELSH OFFICE (1987). *National Curriculum: Task Group on Assessment and Testing - A Report.* London: HMSO

LOEVINGER, J. (1947), *A Systematic Approach to the Construction and Evaluation ofTests ofAbility.* Washington: American Psychological Association

Symposium Participants
Friday 10th September 1993

Chairman

Ray Sumner, NFER

Speakers

Dylan Wiliam, King's College London

Diane Shorrocks and Nick Nelson, University of Leeds

Ann Filer, West of England University

Alastair Pollitt, Cambridge University

Ian Schagen, NFER

Dougal Hutchison, NFER

Discussants

Caroline Gipps, President, BERA

Rob Taylor, SEAC

Tom Christie, Manchester University

GLOSSARY OF TERMS

Term (Abbreviation)	Definition
aggregation	The process of deriving a single Level for an AT based on multiple inputs, usually SoA or item results. The term is also used for the process of deriving subject Levels from multiple AT Levels.
attainment target (AT)	Each subject is subdivided into one or more ATs, each comprising up to ten Levels of attainment, each characterised by SoAs.
ENCA	Evaluation of National Curriculum Assessment — a project based at Leeds University to evaluate the 1991 KS1 assessment, using specialised detailed testing instruments.
IRT	Item Response Theory, a way of modelling item and pupil characteristics with a long history and much software based upon it.
key stage (KS1, KS2, KS3, KS4)	Period of compulsory schooling, consisting of several National Curriculum years. Assessment of each child is to be carried out and reported at the end of each key stage. The abbreviations KS1, KS2 etc. are often used for Key Stage 1, Key Stage 2 etc.
Level	One of the ten divisions of attainment into which each AT and subject is divided, with attainment increasing from Level 1 to Level 10. Pupils who do not achieve Level 1 are classified as 'W'.
National Curriculum (NC)	The edifice of core and foundation subjects and their assessment introduced in the 1988 Education Reform Act.
National Curriculum Assessment (NCA)	The process of deriving a Level for each pupil in every AT and subject at the end of a key stage. This has two strands — teacher assessment (TA) and (for some ATs) statutory tests or tasks.

NCC	National Curriculum Council, responsible for overseeing the National Curriculum and its development. Since October 1993 its responsibilities have been taken over by SCAA.
NFER	National Foundation for Educational Research.
NRT	Norm-referenced testing, as opposed to criterion-referenced testing (CRT), of which NCA is an example. In NRT pupils are ranked in order relative to their peers, usually based on a total score of correct items.
SCAA	School Curriculum and Assessment Authority, formed in 1993 to combine the responsibilities of the NCC and SEAC.
SEAC	School Examinations and Assessment Council, responsible for developing and overseeing NCA. Since October 1993 its responsibilities have been taken over by SCAA.
standard assessment task (SAT)	An element of the statutory NCA applied at the end of a key stage, comprising standard activities to be assessed in the classroom and providing evidence of attainment on a number of SoAs for one or more ATs.
statement of attainment (SoA)	For each AT at every Level, one or more SoAs are defined by statute, which represent the criteria which must be achieved to be awarded the Level.
teacher assessment (TA)	Assessment of pupils relative to the Levels of each AT carried out by teachers on an ongoing basis, not involving the use of statutory tests.
TGAT	Task Group on Assessment and Testing, which reported on assessment procedures before the 1988 Education Reform Act, and which introduced most of the basic concepts currently underlying NCA.

CHAIRMAN'S COMMENTS

Ray Sumner
National Foundation for Educational Research

The measurement-focused title for this symposium would have been 'The reliability of National Curriculum tests and assessments'; one which might have implied that reliability was determinate rather than problematic. As the papers and commentaries in this booklet illustrate, however, reliability in the National Curriculum contexts is not a simple matter of applying the well-tried techniques to produce indices which induce qualified confidence in the assessment results. The peculiar structure of the NC obliged the teachers and those devising the assessments to accept unprecedented constraints which, especially for the tests, have posed many new questions. The contributors show how they have responded, by re-examining both norm- and criterion- referenced assessment theory and, in some instances, exploring innovative alternatives.

Undoubtedly, these efforts are worthwhile. To the assessment professionals, producing dependable measures is an ethical matter; and it would be equally ethical to recommend discontinuation of any assessments that yielded inaccurate or inconsistent measures. These considerations seemingly carry little weight with Government ministers committed irrevocably to the generation of league tables, though, ironically, in most circumstances, variability due to error is less of a problem for grouped results except when numbers are small. But it would be cavalier to persist with using assessments that did not yield dependable individual measures; and the requirements are quite stringent (and well-known). The NC Level to which a pupil is assigned ideally should not be affected by the particular task and its associated assessment procedure, the teacher who evaluates the pupil's performance, the conditions under which it is exercised, or the process linking performance with Level.

Intentionally, those most affected by the outcomes from the measures are the pupils. The measurement professionals, of course, know that there will inevitably be some pupils assigned to the wrong Levels, as no measure can be perfect. The central tenet of the NC is progression through a curriculum defined by Levels. In discussion at the symposium, it was remarked that the pupils who would suffer most from erroneous classification would be those placed at a higher Level than their true performance would warrant. Those placed at a lower than true Level would be assessed again in due course and would be reinstated, as it were. The quest for enhanced reliability should, it was suggested, be focused on eliminating the false high gradings. As informed parents might be just as dissatisfied by progression withheld as by falsely ascribed progression, this aspect is debatable. Undoubtedly, teachers who believed they were dealing with misclassified pupils would be placed in a dilemma, particularly so if the SAT and TA were coincident. Neither would headteachers or governors feel satisfied with imputed under-classification of any pupils.

Regrettably, the rigidity of the assessment system in England and Wales may be retained for all but Key Stage 1, so that formal re-assessment would not be possible, nor would results obtained after the deadline for official returns come into the performance indicator figures for classes, schools or LEAs. It is to be hoped that SCAA will prove to be less rigid than its policy-dominated predecessor and issue guidance to teachers which (1) would encourage re-assessment following a period in which a child's performance in class or homework tends to disprove either the SAT or TA results and (2) accept that only the teacher assessment can provide anything like coverage of the curriculum experienced by a pupil. Thus, the prescribed tests would provide standardised reference levels along the lines proposed by the TGAT, and help to reduce inter-teacher variability. However, one of the papers issues a reminder that teachers themselves may not be sufficiently consistent.

Appraisal of NC assessments has been hampered by uncertainties about the model of assessment to be implemented. Using a two-wheeled analogy, Mark 1 was the Black mountain bike, a multi-purpose vehicle which with intensive training might well have yielded cross-validated results. The design was condemned as too expensive and elaborate. What emerged as Mark 2 was the Clarke penny farthing, a monster driven by testing with teacher assessment trailing behind. Though intended to be uni-directional, its path was erratic and many of those who tried to propel it fell off exhausted. Mark 3, its successor, was the Griffiths bone shaker. As this stopped when it was pushed too hard, it was not possible to assess its reliability. For Mark 4, a new designer has been engaged. Thus the Dearing might become a foldaway runabout, a slimmed down Mark 1 with testing geared to calibrate a bearable load of teacher assessment.

But national tests or assessments are no joke. Their consequences are far-reaching, extending, for instance, to the parent-child relationship and parent-teacher interaction, as well as the public perception of a school. Little is known, apart from hearsay, about what parents say or do when they have been given NC Assessment information or results for their child. Neither has there been any inquiry into pupils' understanding of the system and how their self-regard may be influenced by knowledge of their results. Needless to say, measures that are not wholly dependable introduce another dimension into these dynamics, the importance of which has so far been ignored.

It is no criticism of the contributors to this BERA symposium to comment that all but one of the papers is focused on the technicalities of evaluating reliability. Given the short but erratic history of the NC Assessment, affected by doctrinaire and teacher-parental pressures, with studies hemmed in by contractual restrictions on communication, it is hardly surprising that research has been trammelled in this way. However, the commentaries point to certain fundamental questions that should also be addressed. The open and consultative style newly established by SCAA will, optimistically, allow for a more comprehensive approach to investigating the technical, pedagogical and relational aspects of assessment variability.

CHAPTER 1

THE STRUCTURE OF NATIONAL CURRICULUM ASSESSMENT

Marian Sainsbury

National Foundation for Educational Research

The National Curriculum (NC) was introduced into England and Wales as a result of the 1988 Education Act. It was ambitious in its scope, covering both curriculum content and assessment arrangements and applying to all pupils in maintained schools between the ages of 5 and 16. Its introduction was planned to be phased over a number of years; but in addition to this planned phasing, it soon became clear that revisions were needed to elements that had already been introduced. The history of the first few years of the National Curriculum is therefore one of changes, and sometimes changes upon changes. This chapter will set the scene for the other papers in the book by outlining the structure of the National Curriculum and its assessment arrangements, and by tracing through the first few years those developments that are relevant to the other papers. At the time of writing, a review of the entire curriculum and its assessment arrangements is being undertaken by Sir Ron Dearing at the Government's request and a new agency, the School Curriculum and Assessment Authority (SCAA), has been set up to oversee development. It can therefore be assumed that further changes will follow from 1994 onwards.

The National Curriculum

The 1988 legislation set in place the framework of a ten-subject curriculum and assessment arrangements which are directly related to it. Central to the curriculum are the three **core subjects**, English (or Welsh), mathematics and science. Then, there are seven compulsory **foundation subjects**: technology, history, geography, art, music, physical education and (from the age of 11 only) a modern foreign language. Each of these subjects has **programmes of study**, which define what is to be taught, but do not attempt to prescribe teaching methods. A new agency, the National Curriculum Council (NCC), was set up at the time of the Act and continued until 1993 to oversee and support the curricular elements of the legislation.

Alongside the programmes of study, each subject has **attainment targets (ATs).** These represent a body of knowledge, skills and understanding within the subject. The structure of the attainment targets within the core subjects is set out in Table 1. It will be clear from this table that there were fundamental changes to the structure of both mathematics and science after only two years of the system: 14 mathematics attainment targets were reduced to five; and 17 in science reduced to only four. The programmes of study for both subjects, however, remained the same; the new attainment targets simply represented a change in the grouping of the subject matter. These new attainment targets were introduced in 1991, but assessed for the first time only in 1992 or 1993. Most of the papers in this book refer to the old targets. In English, the original attainment targets remain (for the moment) unchanged. A proposal for a radical rewriting of this subject was put forward early in 1993, but was then superseded ... ssment review.

... Curriculum

... new curriculum were proposed in 1987 by ... roup on Assessment and Testing (TGAT), ... rom 1988-1993 by the School Examinations ... he aim was to provide an assessment system ... se were that it should be:

- ... mation on where a pupil is, enabling teachers ...

- ... verall information on the achievement of ...

- evaluative — providing aggregated information on classes and schools to assess curriculum issues, as well as the functioning of teachers and schools;

- informative — providing information to parents about their own children and general information about the school;

- for professional development — giving teachers greater sophistication in assessment, recording and monitoring so that they can evaluate their own work.

To meet these objectives, TGAT proposed the innovative assessment system that forms the subject of this book (GB.DES, 1988). Attainment is measured on a continuous scale of ten Levels, covering the entire 5 to 16 age range. The **ten-Level scale** is a criterion-referenced scale. Each Level is defined by a set of criteria known as **statements of attainment (SoAs)**. Pupils attain a level by demonstrating the performance set out in the criteria. This differs fundamentally from the more traditional norm-referenced test model, where pupils are ranked in order in comparison to others of their age.

Table 2 sets out as an example the ten Levels of old Attainment Target 3 in mathematics, which covered number operations. This demonstrates the progressive nature of the ten-Level scale, and the relationships of statements of attainment within a Level, in a fairly limited and well-defined subject domain, and thus exemplifies the principles of this assessment model. Since the earliest days of National Curriculum Assessment, a standard form of abbreviation has been used, and this occurs in some of the later chapters: **Ma 3/2c** means mathematics Attainment Target 3, Level 2, Statement c.

The attainment targets in each subject and the statements of attainment defining each level were determined by separate working groups of experts in each subject. Thus the criteria do not represent empirical findings about pupils' attainments, but rather the judgements of the working groups.

From this description of the overall assessment system, the central concerns of this book may be discerned. How can a National Curriculum Level be derived from the defining criteria? On what evidence should assessments be based? How much confidence can be placed in these Levels?

The assessment system consists of two separate and complementary strands. On the one hand, there is continuous assessment by teachers, known as **teacher assessment (TA)**, and, on the other, assessment by externally devised **assessment tasks or tests**. Teacher assessment always includes all attainment targets, but the tasks and tests may cover only selected targets. Both of these strands are discussed in more detail below.

Ages and key stages

The legislation set out four ages at which pupils should be externally assessed according to National Curriculum criteria. These are the ages of **7, 11, 14 and 16.** Each corresponds to the end of a **key stage** (KS) of education, lasting for two, three or four school years. Table 3 sets out the ages of the pupils, the school years — now running continuously through the 5-16 range — and the key stages. Figure 1 shows the range of Levels that pupils might be expected to attain at the end of each key stage.

The timetable for the introduction of the curriculum and statutory assessment followed a cohort of children as they started the primary or the secondary phase of their education. Children aged five started on the National Curriculum in 1989, and were then assessed when they reached the end of Key Stage 1, in 1991. Similarly, children aged 11 started on the National Curriculum in 1989, and were first assessed when they reached the end of Key Stage 3, in 1992. Table 4 shows this timetable in more detail.

Figure 1: Sequence of pupil achievement of levels between ages 7 and 16

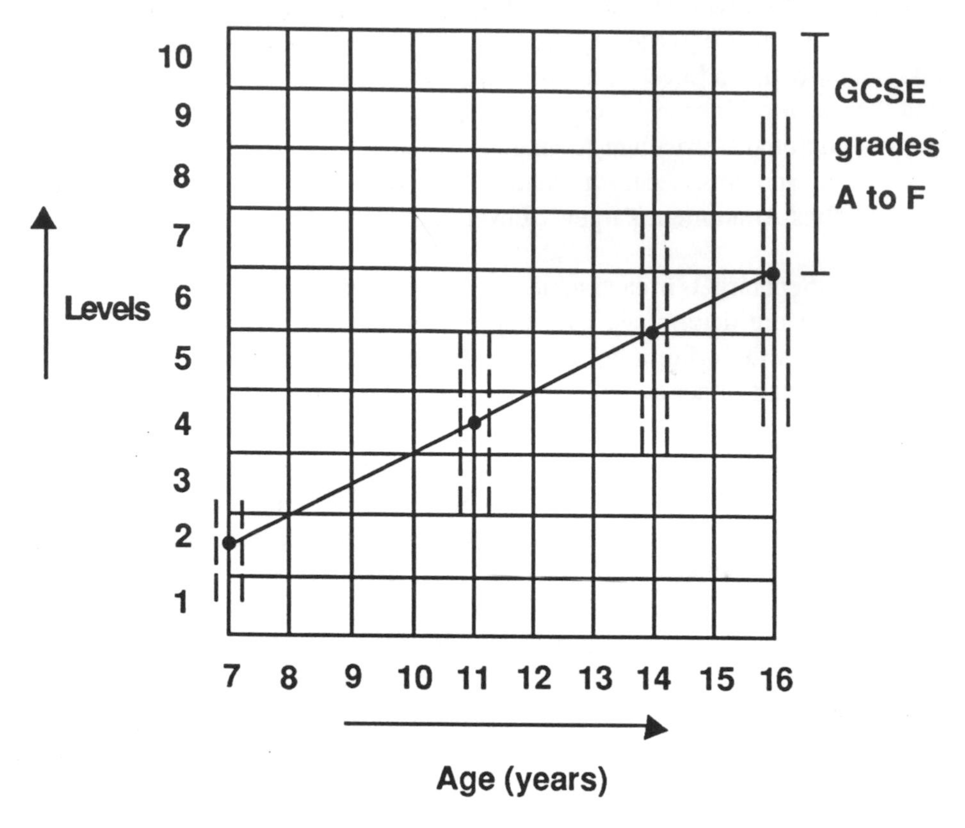

Teacher assessment

As teachers go about teaching the National Curriculum programmes of study, they are required to make assessments of what children have learned. How they do this is a matter for individual teachers and schools to decide: there is no statutory requirement to use any particular approach to assessment or to recording. The main purpose of this is a formative one, to ensure that future teaching is well matched to what children already know.

There is an assumption that these continuous assessments will be informed and structured by the statements of attainment, but there is not, and has never been, a requirement that teachers should keep records against each statement. A variety of practices has grown up for making continuous records of children's attainment. Many schools have used a recording system based on statements of attainment, but often with more detail. Individual pupil portfolios are widely used, and optional materials have been produced by SEAC/SCAA to support assessment.

At the end of each key stage, teachers are also required to make a formal assessment of the Level attained by each child in each attainment target. In this formal teacher assessment, they are expected to have regard to the content of the statements of attainment, and to have evidence to back up their judgements. But they are not required to make an assessment of each statement, only of the overall Level. It is open to teachers to make global judgements of Level, or to assess each statement of attainment separately.

This formal procedure had to be completed by the end of March in 1991, the first year of the system. Teachers found it difficult to cover the entire programmes of study by this date, and in subsequent years the teacher assessment date was later, at the end of May in 1992, and in mid-June in 1993.

Standard assessment tasks and National Curriculum tests

To complement the teacher assessment strand, there are externally devised assessment instruments of various types. These have changed radically from year to year since their introduction, and are variously described as tasks or tests, according to the approach taken.

The notion of a **standard assessment task** originated with the TGAT report. The aim was to develop a new kind of assessment instrument, which would be broader in its scope than traditional tests, and would allow the assessment of practical and problem-solving skills as well as knowledge and understanding. Some of these tasks would be relatively formal, but others would be informal classroom activities. Research projects were set up by SEAC in 1989 to devise such tasks for Key Stages 1 and 3.

In 1990, there was a national pilot for Key Stage 1 assessments. Three development agencies piloted a wide range of tasks. Most of these were cross-curricular and thematically based, to reflect common practice in the curriculum with children of this age. The aim was to cover all attainment targets, but even at this stage it was clear that there was too much subject-matter for full coverage to be possible.

The first statutory national assessment was in 1991, also with Key Stage 1, the seven-year-olds. Teachers had to use standard tasks to assess nine attainment targets across the three subjects. In English, these were reading, writing, spelling and handwriting; in mathematics, using and applying mathematics, number, and one other from a choice of four; in science, exploration of science and one other from a choice of three. Only Levels 1-3 were covered. In some tasks, all children attempted all Levels; in others, entry and exit points were provided so that only appropriate Levels of work were attempted. These standard assessment tasks became known by the abbreviation SATs, which is still commonly used, although the Government and SEAC ceased to use it after 1992.

These tasks formed a formidable, and ultimately unacceptable, workload for teachers, for a number of reasons. The requirement to assess was entirely new to teachers of children of this age, and the structure of the attainment targets was complex and detailed. There was a wide range of subject matter to be covered in total. Two of the attainment targets in particular, exploration of science and using and applying mathematics, were assessed by means of practical tasks which were often extremely time-consuming. Teachers were advised to work with small groups of children, because of the practical nature of much of the work, and those with large classes had to repeat the tasks many times.

The 1992 standard tasks for Key Stage 1 therefore retreated from the broad TGAT model and instead used worksheets for most of the assessments, so that children responded mainly in writing and could work in larger groups. Only seven attainment targets were assessed, and the two most time-consuming, practical mathematics and science, were excluded. This model changed little in 1993, except that the mathematics and science targets were the new ones.

At Key Stage 3, the assessments for 14-year-olds were also originally envisaged as broadly based standard tasks, but later the direction of development was changed, and the final pilot materials used in 1992 and 1993 were formal tests in the three core subjects.

The assessments at Key Stage 2 followed a later timetable, so that children assessed at 11 would have followed the National Curriculum for their entire school career. The first national pilot took place in 1993, and is to be followed by a second national pilot in 1994. By the time the Key Stage 2 specification was drawn up, the emphasis was firmly upon formal tests rather than broadly based tasks.

In 1993, the entire National Curriculum Assessment system was undermined by a teachers' boycott, which originated at Key Stage 3 but spread widely amongst other teachers, based on claims of excessive workload and doubts about the nature of some of the tests. This disrupted the Key Stage 3 tests and some aspects of the Key Stage 1 assessments, and reduced the scope of the Key Stage 2 pilot to such an extent that it was necessary to repeat it the following year. The review by Sir Ron Dearing is in response to these concerns.

Aggregation

With a criterion-referenced system such as this, there are important questions about what constitutes 'mastery' at a Level. Should all the statements be attained? Each more than once? Or should some allowance be made for careless mistakes or inconsistent performance?

Within the system described, there are several answers to these questions, one for teacher assessment and others for standard tasks and tests. In teacher assessment, as described above, there is no requirement to apply any particular rule; teachers may, if they wish, make a global, or even impressionistic assessment of a child's Level. They should have evidence to back this up, which may be inspected by a local moderator.

In the standard tasks, however, a rule is necessary. At Key Stage 1, teachers record an assessment of each statement of attainment, almost all of which are included in the tasks. These are then aggregated to arrive at a Level, using a rule known as **'n or n-1'**:

- if there is one statement assessed, it must be attained
- if there are two statements assessed, both must be attained
- if there are three or more statements assessed, all or all but one must be attained.

Once the attainment target Level has been decided, further rules, some of them involving weightings, must be applied to derive the Level for the entire subject. The old attainment targets had an intermediate grouping, the **profile component**, which consisted of a number of related attainment targets within a subject. This no longer applies for the new attainment targets.

At Key Stages 2 and 3, the pilot materials have used a variety of systems for awarding Levels. Since these are tests giving rise to a total score, it is possible to assign a Level from the total score alone, or to use scores within levels, or to base the assessment on statements of attainment. The Level awarded can be for an attainment target, or for the subject overall. All these approaches have been tried, and final decisions have yet to be made about the system to be used in the future.

References

GREAT BRITAIN. DEPARTMENT OF EDUCATION AND SCIENCE AND WELSH OFFICE (1988). *National Curriculum: Task Group on Assessment and Testing. A Report*. London: DES.

Table 1: The structure of the attainment targets in the core subjects

English

En1	Speaking and listening
En2	Reading
En3	Writing
En4	Spelling
En5	Handwriting

Mathematics - 1989

Ma1	Using and applying mathematics
Ma2	Number
Ma3	Number (Operations)
Ma4	Number (Estimation)
Ma5	Number/Algebra
Ma6	Algebra
Ma7	Algebra (Graphical representation)
Ma8	Measures
Ma9	Using and applying mathematics
Ma10	Shape and space (Shapes)
Ma11	Shape and space (Location)
Ma12	Handling data (Collecting and recording)
Ma13	Handling data (Representing and interpreting)
Ma14	Handling data (Probabilities)

1991

Ma1	Using and applying mathematics
Ma2	Number
Ma3	Algebra
Ma4	Shape and space
Ma5	Handling data

Science - 1989

Sc1	Exploration of science
Sc2	The variety of life
Sc3	Processes of life
Sc4	Genetics and evolution
Sc5	Human influences on the Earth
Sc6	Types and uses of materials
Sc7	Making new materials
Sc8	Explaining how materials behave
Sc9	Earth and atmosphere
Sc10	Forces
Sc11	Electricity and magnetism
Sc12	Information technology and microelectronics
Sc13	Energy
Sc14	Sound and music
Sc15	Using light and electromagnetic radiation
Sc16	The Earth in space
Sc17	The nature of science

1991

Sc1	Scientific investigation
Sc2	Life and living processes
Sc3	Materials and their properties
Sc4	Physical processes

Table 2: Ma3 (Number: Operations)

LEVEL	STATEMENTS OF ATTAINMENT
	Pupils should:
1	• add or subtract using objects where the numbers involved are no greater than 10.
2	• know and use addition and subtraction facts up to 10.
	• compare two numbers to find the difference.
	• solve whole number problems involving addition and subtraction, including money.
3	• know and use addition and subtraction number facts to 20 (including zero).
	• solve problems involving multiplication or division of whole numbers or money, using a calculator where necessary.
	• know and use multiplication facts up to 5 x 5, and all those in 2, 5 and 10 multiplication tables.
4	• know multiplication facts up to 10 x 10 and use them in multiplication and division problems.
	• (using whole numbers) add or subtract mentally two 2-digit numbers; add mentally several single-digit numbers; without a calculator add and subtract two 3-digit numbers, multiply a 2-digit number by a single-digit number and divide a 2-digit number by a single- digit number.
	• solve addition or subtraction problems using numbers with no more than two decimal places; solve multiplication or division problems starting with whole numbers.
5	• (using whole numbers) understand and use non-calculator methods by which a 3-digit number is multiplied by a 2-digit number and a 3-digit number is divided by a 2-digit number.
	• calculate fractions and percentages of quantities using a calculator where necessary.
	• multiply and divide mentally single-digit multiples of powers of 10 with whole number answers.
	• use negative numbers in context.
6	• work out fractional and percentage changes and related calculations.
	• calculate using ratios in a variety of situations.
	• convert fractions to decimals and percentages and find one number as a percentage of another.
7	• multiply and divide mentally single digit multiples of any power of 10, and realise that, with a number less than 1, multiplication has a decreasing effect and division has an increasing effect.
	• solve multiplication and division problems involving numbers of any size.
	• use the memory and bracket facility of a calculator to plan a calculation and evaluate expressions.
8	• calculate with numbers in standard form (with positive and negative powers of 10).
	• substitute negative numbers into formulae involving addition, subtraction, multiplication and division.
	• calculate with fractions.
9	• use the knowledge, skills and understanding attained at lower levels in a wider range of contexts.
10	• use the knowledge, skills and understanding attained at lower levels in a wider range of contexts.

Table 3: Ages, school years and key stages

	Age	School year
	4 - 5	Reception
Key Stage 1		
	5 - 6	1
	6 - 7	2
Key Stage 2		
	7 - 8	3
	8 - 9	4
	9 -10	5
	10 -11	6
Key Stage 3		
	11 - 12	7
	12 - 13	8
	13 - 14	9
Key Stage 4		
	14 - 15	10
	15 - 16	11

Note: the school year runs from 1 September to 31 August. Within this period, all the children in a year group will have a birthday, on which they attain the higher age listed. Thus, children in Year 1 will all start the school year aged five, and all have their sixth birthday in the course of that school year.

Table 4: Timetable for the introduction of the National Curriculum (core subjects)

School Year	Key Stage 1	Key Stage 2	Key Stage 3
1989/90	Programmes of study Pilot assessment		Programmes of study(Ma,Sc)
1990/91	Statutory assessment	Programmes of study	Programmes of study (Ma,Sc,En) Pilot assessment (Ma, Sc, En)
1991/92	Statutory assessment	Programmes of study	Programmes of study Pilot assessment
1992/93	Statutory assessment	Programmes of study Pilot assessment	Statutory assessment
1993/94	Statutory assessment	Pilot assessment	Statutory assessment

(At Key Stage 4, the introduction of assessment has been delayed to resolve problems of comparability with the existing GCSE system.)

CHAPTER 2

RECONCEPTUALISING VALIDITY, DEPENDABILITY AND RELIABILITY FOR NATIONAL CURRICULUM ASSESSMENT

Dylan Wiliam, King's College London

Introduction

This paper is an attempt to contribute the process of reconceptualising the notions of validity, dependability and reliability for use in the evaluation of National Curriculum Assessment.

The first section outlines briefly the historical development of the idea of validity. The focus placed by current definitions of construct validity – as the extent to which inferences based on assessment outcomes are warranted – is then used in the second section to develop analogous definitions for reliability and dependability. The third section looks at traditional formulations of reliability and dependability, which were designed for use with continuous mark scales, and discusses some of the features of the traditional definitions that render them inappropriate for the kinds of dichotomous attributions that are required in National Curriculum Assessment.

The final section presents a basic outline of signal detection theory which was developed originally in communication engineering to describe the performance of systems in making dichotomous judgements in response to continuously variable signals. It is argued that such an approach is far more appropriate for the evaluation of the reliability and dependability of National Curriculum Assessments than that offered by classical test theory, and two illustrations of the application of the theory to questions in National Curriculum Assessment are given.

The technical foundations of validity

The most common definition, and one which continues to abound in introductory texts on the subject, is that it is the extent to which 'it measures what it purports to measure' (Garrett, 1937, p324). In a similar vein, Anastasi (1990) describes the validity of a test as being concerned with '*what* the test measures and *how well* it does so' (p139 – emphasis in original).

However, such a definition, while giving some idea of the what validity is about, does not lend itself readily to operational definitions. Accordingly, over the past 50 or so years, many authors have proposed different definitions of validity, emphasising different facets of the central concept. Indeed, by 1980 it was estimated that there were over 30 different types of validity in the literature (Brown, 1980). Some of the more important of these are discussed below – a more detailed account of this development can be found in Wiliam (1993).

Content and descriptive validity

A test that claims to assess a particular domain has content validity to the extent that the content of the test is both *relevant* to the domain addressed, and *complete*, in that all important aspects of the domain are addressed. In the past, content validation was simply a question of the relationship between an assessment and its title, with the implication is that once validated, a test is validated for all time.

However, there are occasions when the test questions seem to be content-valid, but the answers given by students challenge this assumption. For example, the validity of a test designed to assess students' understanding of history would be in question if students with poor reading ability, but a good understanding of history, obtained low marks.

The important distinction here is between *bias* and *impact*. We have (at least) two variables: the variable in which we are interested (historical understanding), called the *focal* variable, and another variable (or variables), called the *nuisance* variable(s) (Ackerman, 1991, p69). The test can have a different *impact* on two groups (fluent readers and non-fluent readers) without calling into question its validity. The test is *biased* only if the two groups differed in terms of the nuisance variable but *not* on the focal variable. In our example, the history test appears to be valid for fluent readers, but shows bias for poor readers.

Popham (1978) coined the term descriptive validity to emphasise further that validation should focus attention on whether the assessment described the subject's behaviour, and therefore could not be judged from the test alone. Formally, descriptive validity is the extent to which an assessment is actually measuring what its descriptive scheme contends it is measuring. Popham also pointed out that this term clearly admits assessments of the affective and psychomotor domains, which appear to be excluded by the term 'content validity'. However, subsequently, Popham (1981, p100) 'retracted' the term in order to avoid contributing to the proliferation of kinds of validity.

Criterion-related validity

Although assessments are sometimes administered simply in order to find out about a candidates' competence in a particular domain, they are more often administered in order to make decisions, and in particular to predict the candidate's performance on some criterion. Sometimes, the criterion relates to future performance, such as 'will this person make a good doctor?' so that the *predictive* aspect of validity is paramount. At other times, the ability of the assessment to deliver the same result as some other more complex procedure is more important, so that validation is more concerned with the extent to which the result of the assessment is *concurrent* with the more complex procedure. Because both predictive validity and concurrent validity are questions about the ability of the assessment to predict performance on some criterion, they are often referred to collectively as criterion-related validity.

The important point about criterion-related validity is that it is not a property of the assessment itself, but of the use to which information from the test is put – a test is never valid, only valid for a particular purpose (Wood, 1985, p136).

The idea that validity should be more concerned with the inferences made from assessment results, rather than the results themselves was made more explicit in the development, during the 1950s, of *construct* validity.

Construct validity

The term *construct validity* was first introduced in 1954 by a joint committee of the American Psychological Association, the American Educational Research Association and the National Council on Measurement Used in Education (1954) and elaborated in the following year (Cronbach and Meehl, 1955).

The paper by Cronbach and Meehl also sought to locate construct validity within an explicitly scientific framework, and a substantial proportion of the paper is devoted to 'the logic of construct validation' which presents a view of the philosophy of science that is appropriate to construct validity.

The key to the logic of construct validation is the idea of a *nomological network*, which is described as the 'interlocking system of laws which constitute a theory' (p290). These laws deal with observable properties and theoretical constructs, and consist of relationships between properties, or between constructs, or relationships between properties and constructs. In addition, each nomological net must include some observable properties, in order to 'permit predictions about events' (Cronbach and Meehl, 1955, p290) – in other words to generate what Popper (1963) called 'falsifiable' propositions – because '*unless the network makes contact with observations, and exhibits explicit, public steps of inference, construct validation cannot be claimed*' (Cronbach and Meehl, 1955, p291 – emphasis in original).

In this context, there are two major problems with exhibiting 'explicit public steps of inference'. The first is that even within a subject as precisely defined as mathematics, it is now acknowledged that there are severe difficulties is establishing what, exactly, constitutes a justification or a 'warrant' for belief (Kitcher, 1984). The second is that these problems are compounded in the social sciences because the chain of inference, as Cronbach and Meehl conceded, might have to be probabilistic, rather than deterministic. In this case, the traditional definition of 'knowledge' – as justified-true-belief (Griffiths, 1967) – is of even less help, because the assertion may justified, but not true!

There is, however, a secondary requirement in construct validation, which suggests a partial solution to the problem of inference. As well as using a nomological net to support the intended interpretation of the assessment outcomes, construct validation also requires the *elimination of rival plausible hypotheses*. In other words, not only is it incumbent on the user of assessment results to establish that the intended interpretation is justified, but the user must also establish that no other (substantially different) interpretations are as justifiable.

The approach suggested by Goldman (1976) for the basis of perceptual knowledge has as its central feature the idea that knowing something is, in essence, the ability to eliminate other rival possibilities.

For example, if a person, (let us call her or him Chris) sees a book in a school, then we are likely to say that Chris knows it is a book. However, if we know (but Chris does not) that students at this school are expert in making replica books that, to all external appearances, look like books but are solid and cannot be opened, then with a justified-true-belief view of knowledge, we would say that Chris does not *know* it is a book, even if it is.

Goldman rejects both non-accidentality (Unger, 1968) – i.e. that the belief was not arrived at accidentally – and indefeasibility (Klein, 1971; Lehrer and Paxson, 1969) – i.e. that the justification for the belief has not been defeated – as a basis for resolving this dilemma.

Instead, he proposes that Chris knows that the object in sight is a book if it is discriminable or distinguishable by her or him from a relevant possible state of affairs in which it is not a book. If, on the other hand, there *is* a relevant possible state of affairs which Chris cannot distinguish from the actual state of affairs, then Chris cannot be said to know. In this sense, knowing is independent of the knowers. In our example, if we know that the replica books do exist in that school, then we would deny that Chris knows that the object is a book.

This need to distinguish among possible relevant states of affairs seems to offer a workable framework for construct validity, although, as Goldman concedes, a large part of the burden of definition falls on the definition of the word 'relevant'. Construct validation consists of the dual process of establishing that the preferred interpretation is warranted by the evidence, and also that there is no other relevant state of affairs in which an alternative interpretation is more warranted.

Such a process can never be completed and there are no 'off-the-peg methodologies'; only a never-ending process of *marshalling evidence to support the assertion that a particular inference is warranted on the basis of the assessment results*, and what is validated is the *meaning* of assessment results.

It is clear therefore that 'One does not validate a test, but only a principle for making inferences' (Cronbach and Meehl, 1955, p297) or 'an interpretation of data arising from a specified procedure' (Cronbach, 1971).

Nearly forty years ago, Jane Loevinger had asserted that 'since predictive, concurrent, and content validities are all essentially *ad hoc*, construct validity is the whole of validity from a scientific point of view (Loevinger, 1957, p636) and Angoff (1988 p28) notes that by the late 1970s, there was increasing agreement with the view that, to all intents and purposes, construct validity subsumed all other aspects of validity.

However, this agreement was not universal. Bechtoldt (1959) was critical of construct validity because it determined the meaning of a score from its relationship with what it predicts or signifies. This distinction was expanded by Embretson (1983) into the distinction between construct representation and nomothetic span. For Embretson,

> *construct representation concerns identifying the theoretical constructs (e.g. components, strategies, and knowledge structures) that are involved in responding to the specific items that appear on the test. These variables, obviously, are central to cognitive psychology, and assessing them requires applying the methods of experimental cognitive psychology to test items. Nomothetic span, in contrast concerns the utility of the test as a measure of individual differences. Nomothetic span includes the relationship of test scores to other measures and to individual differences in the underlying components, strategies and knowledge structures. Applying Bechtoldt' distinction, construct representation concerns the meaning of scores, whereas nomothetic span concerns the significance of scores* (Embretson, 1992, pp 126-127).

However, despite these criticisms of the way that aspects of validity are partitioned, it is clear that the notion of validity had broadened from:

- a property of an assessment (content validity); *to* -
- a property of the behaviours elicited by an assessment (content validity/ descriptive validity); *to* -
- a property of the inferences made on the basis of the assessment (construct validity).

The meaning and consequences of assessment

The analysis presented so far does not take account of the fact that all assessments are conducted on, by, and for individuals who interact in essentially social ways, and, in particular, that the introduction of an assessment may change the way that they interact.

Messick (1980) addressed this by locating all such inferences firmly within the social settings in which they are made. As well as the meanings attached to assessment outcomes, he argues that the process of validation must also consider:

a) evidence for the relevance of the construct and the utility of the particular applications;

b) the value implications of the test interpretation; and

c) the social consequences of the proposed assessment and the use of the results.

He presents this view of validation as the result of a crossing of basis (i.e. evidential or consequential) with function (i.e. result interpretation and result use). This relationship is shown diagrammatically in Figure 1.

Figure 1: Messick's framework for the validation of assessments

		FUNCTION	
		Result interpretation	Result use
BASIS	Evidential basis	construct validity	construct validity & relevance/utility
	Consequential basis	value implications	social consequences

Within this framework, it is possible to see that a consideration of the effects of the use of assessment outcomes on the subsequent behaviour of agents is also part of the validation process. For example, the social pressure to achieve good marks for students may lead a teacher to an undesirable concentration on only those aspects of the curriculum that are to be assessed. Consideration of consequences such as these is sometimes termed 'backwash validation', i.e. the extent to which the assessment 'washes' back into the curriculum.

The classical view, espoused for example by Tyler (1934), is that this is the 'wrong way round' and that 'measurement of classroom achievement has been viewed as an activity that flows from and takes its direction from instruction' (Airasian, 1988 p6). An alternative view – that espoused by adherents to measurement-driven instruction (MDI) – is that since the test lays out a series of expectations as to what is regarded as important, then in certain circumstances *not* teaching to the test would be less in the students' interests than teaching to the test (Airasian, 1987).

It is only with this widest of all possible theoretical frameworks that an adequate analysis of thc validity of National Curriculum Assessment can be undertaken, and in particular, there will be a continuing tension between the meaning (the evidential basis of validity) and consequences (the consequential basis) of National Curriculum Assessment.

Reliability and dependability

When we make assessments, we are hardly ever interested primarily in the actual items we are testing – we are interested in the ability of the assessment result to 'speak' for other aspects not tested. Assessment information is useful because we believe that we can generalise from the actual items assessed to some wider domain and validity can thus be regarded as 'the degree to which the responses to an assessment can be generalised' (Nuttall, 1987, p110).

For example, a short test of basic arithmetic might be administered to a cohort of students in a school. From the results, different inferences might be made involving different degrees of generalisation. The least general inference is probably that if the students took the same test again, they would each get a similar mark on each occasion. This is a question of test-retest reliability, or reliability as the *stability* of the result.

A slightly more general inference is possible is we know that the marks would be roughly the same if, instead of administering the same test twice, we administered two similar matched tests (i.e. two parallel forms of the same test). If we insist that each item in the second test mirrors an item in the first test, then we are still, in a way measuring the *stability* of the test rcsult. This aspect of reliability is sometimes called classically-parallel parallel-forms reliability (Feldt and Brennan, 1989).

If, instead of ensuring that each item in one test corresponds to an item in the other, we make both tests a random sample of items from the assessment domain, then we have two *randomly-parallel* tests. If each student gets similar marks on the two tests now, we can make a stronger inference: we can infer that the mark she or he achieves gives us an idea of the extent to which the student has attained (in our example) the skills of basic arithmetic. This is another within-domain inference, but it is more general than is usually associated with the term reliability. The idea of a quantitative index of the *generalizability* of an inference to the whole of the domain from which the sample is drawn was developed by Cronbach and his collaborators during the 1960s (Cronbach,

Rajaratnam, and Gleser, 1963), and culminated in a theory of the *dependability* of behavioural measurements (Cronbach, Gleser, Nanda, and Rajaratnam, 1972).

The relationship between validity, dependability and reliability can therefore be viewed as a nested sequence of domains to which generalisations can be made (Wiliam, 1993):

- validity is the extent to which inferences within and outside the domain of assessment are warranted;
- dependability is the extent to which inferences within the domain of assessment are warranted
- reliability is the extent to which inferences about the parts of the domain *actually* assessed are warranted.

With these definitions, validity therefore covers, in Messick's terms, the evidential basis of both the meaning and the use of assessment results, and in Embretson's terms, both construct representation and nomothetic span. Dependability, on the other hand, concerns only the former aspect of each conceptualisation: in Messick's terms, the evidential basis of the meaning of assessment results, and in Embretson's terms, construct representation.

If content validity is conceptualised as the extent to which the assessment sample is *relevant* to the domain being addressed, and also *covers* the domain, then dependability can be envisaged as the intersection of reliability and content validity. In other words, an assessment is *dependable* to the extent that it is both *content valid* and *reliable*.

Conversely, we can see that reliability is a prerequisite for dependability, and dependability a prerequisite for validity, because if we cannot have faith in the assessment to tell us anything about what was actually assessed, we can have even less faith in generalisations to wider domains.

The strength of the warrant for any inferences will, of course, depend on a number of factors. In the context of National Curriculum Assessment the strength of the warrant for within-domain inferences (i.e. the dependability) is critically affected by three separate processes (Wiliam, 1993):

- an agreed interpretation of the assessment domain is decided, which leads to a well-defined assessment domain;
- the student's attainment with respect to the domain is assessed (with some error); and
- the pattern of a student's successes and failures on the various sub-domains is aggregated to give a small number of scores for reporting purposes.

Clearly if the domain to which an assessments refers is not well-defined, then any inferences about a student's capabilities or achievements within that domain are likely to be flawed. Additionally, if inferences are made about a score that is derived by combining several sub-scores, then the justification for the inferences will depend on the method used for combining the sub-scores. Discussion of these two issues is beyond the scope of this paper, but they are treated in some detail in Wiliam (1992).

Approaches to measuring reliability and dependability

The remainder of this chapter deals with the process of assessing a student's competence with respect to a well-defined domain, and in particular examines the issues involved in classifying students dichotomously as either having achieved the domain, or as not having achieved the domain.

The first part of this section reviews classical reliability theory and the second part demonstrates how such a notion of the reliability of an assessment is not particularly appropriate for National Curriculum Assessment. In the third part, other formulations of reliability based on classification-consistency are considered and in part four, the principles of utility theory to place values on the different kinds of classifications are outlined. In the final part, it is shown how the approaches of decision-consistency and utility theory can be incorporated within a new approach – signal detection theory – which holds considerable promise for the evaluation of assessment systems.

Classical reliability theory

'Classical' reliability theory is an attempt to extend to assessment the idea of the 'signal-to-noise-ratio' developed by Shannon and Weaver (1949) for communication engineering. When we use the results of assessments we want the amount of 'signal' to be large when compared with the amount of 'noise'.

The theory assumes that every observed score that is delivered by an assessment is made up of a true score and an error. The variance of the true scores is used as an index of the total amount of 'signal' and the variance of the errors is used an index of the total amount of 'noise'. The reliability of the assessment is then defined as the ratio of the true-score variance to the observed-score variance.

However, as Cronbach (1947) states:

> *the reliability of a test, as so defined, is a concept which cannot be directly observed* (p2 – emphasis in original).

and so we have to make indirect estimates. This is usually done by obtaining two sets of test results for each individual. These can be from the same test administered twice (reliability as stability), from the odd and even-numbered questions in the same test ('split-half' reliability), from two matched tests (classically parallel forms), or from two tests randomly sampled from the same domain (randomly parallel forms). But as Cronbach points out in the same article:

> *Different assumptions lead to different types of coefficients, which are not estimates of each other* (p2 – emphasis in original).

and goes on to cite studies that have shown that some measures which have high split-half 'reliabilities' have low test-retest 'reliabilities'.

What makes classical reliability theory a single theory rather than a disparate set of theories is that the different formulations of reliability rely on substantially the same set of mathematical derivations, based on the correlations between the two sets of test scores. The details of the theory can be found in any standard text on educational or psychological measurement, but briefly, the theory makes five fundamental assumptions:

1. that the sum of the errors is zero;
2. that error is independent of true score;
3. that the errors on the two sets of observed scores are independent of each other;
4. that each individuals' two true scores are equal;
5. that the two sets of scores have equal error variances.

With these assumptions, it can be shown that the ratio of the true score variance to the observed score variance is the same as the correlation between the two sets of *observed* scores, which gives the usual operational definition of reliability.

Reliability, as traditionally defined, has been very important in the development of educational and psychological assessments, even though there have been many criticisms of the assumptions and definitions. Some of these are taken up in the next section.

Critiques of classical reliability theory

The classical derivation of reliability has been strongly criticised, both on the grounds that the definitions are circular (e.g. true score is defined in terms of parallel forms which are in turn defined in terms of true scores) and that the assumptions are too rarely met in practice for the theory to be relevant. Loevinger (1947) contains a detailed critique of the assumptions of classical reliability theory as well as a brief review of other critiques of the theory, and Seddon (1988) illustrates some of the more bizarre consequences of classical reliability theory.

However, in addition to these general weaknesses, classical reliability theory has particularly unfortunate consequences when used in criterion-referenced assessment systems (Popham and Husek, 1969).

The crucial point is that the concentration on 'signal-to-noise ratio' in classical reliability gives us two ways of improving the reliability. One is to reduce the error variance (i.e. the noise). The other is *by increasing the observed-score variance* (by stretching the candidates out along the mark scale). A test with high reliability may, therefore, simply be one in which the observed-score variance swamps the error variance. However, in criterion-referenced assessments, because of the concentration on achievement, the true-score variance can often be quite small (for example, when teaching is highly successful), and the distribution of errors can be idiosyncratic. A high value of a classical reliability index is therefore neither a necessary nor a sufficient condition for a for a good criterion-referenced assessment.

This illustrates a completely general problem with classical reliability theory and its inflexible approach to the treatment of error: if one knows nothing about the distribution of errors, then one should not be using classical reliability theory, and if one does know something about the distribution of the errors, then one can generally do better.

For this reason, several reformulations of the notion of reliability have been devised for use with criterion-referenced systems, and some of these are considered in the next section.

Decision-consistency approaches to reliability

The original aim of criterion-referenced assessment was to attempt to assign a candidate to one of two mutually exclusive and collectively exhaustive states, usually referred to as 'master' (M) and 'non-master' (NM), but here termed adept (A) and non-adept (NA). Such an assignation might be correct or incorrect, giving a fourfold classification of outcomes:

true adept	a candidate is correctly classified as adept
false adept	a candidate who is a non-adept is incorrectly classified as adept
true non-adept	a candidate is correctly classified as non-adept
false non-adept	a candidate who is adept is incorrectly classified as non-adept.

However, most 'criterion-referenced' assessments use a continuous mark scale, with adept or non-adept status being awarded according to whether the score gained reaches the designated 'cut-score' or not. In National Curriculum Assessment, we may not have an underlying mark scale: a student is regarded as simply achieving or failing to achieve a particular level. In this context, a reliability coefficient is simply an index of decision-consistency for dichotomous decisions (see Subkoviak, 1980).

There are two such indices in widespread use. The first is simply the proportion of persons correctly classified, usually denoted by p, and the second is Cohen's coefficient kappa (Cohen, 1960), defined as:

$$\kappa = \frac{p - p_c}{1 - p_c}$$

where p_c is the proportion of consistent classifications that would be expected by chance. In this sense, kappa is a correction of p in order to account for the fact that even with completely random allocation of candidates to adept and non-adept states, some candidates would be correctly classified purely by chance.

Utility theory

Both of the indices discussed above weight both kinds of mis-classification equally. However, there may be occasions when false-adept attributions 'cost' much more than false-non-adept attributions, such as, for example, the training of airline pilots.

Within educational measurement, the stakes are not likely to be quite so high, but there will be occasions when it is appropriate not to treat false-adept decisions and false non-adept decisions symmetrically. The typical approach has been to set the decision criterion first, and then to derive the various costs and benefits of that particular setting. Such an approach is appropriate when there are strong grounds for setting the interpretation of a criterion in a particular way. However, often, we are concerned with the relative benefits and costs of decisions, and the setting of the interpretation of the criterion needs to take account of this.

An approach to decision-consistency that uses the inherent decision-consistency of the *system*, over a range of possible settings of the criterion, in order to *inform* the standard setting process has been developed from the use of signal detection theory in communication engineering.

Signal detection theory

Signal detection theory (SDT) developed out of attempts to analyse the performance of different (human) receivers of radio signals. However, while having been developed in communication engineering, the idea of dichotomous decision-making in the presence of noise has a very wide range of application (Green and Swets, 1966). For example, workers in social services frequently have to make decisions about whether to take children into care or not. This can be regarded as a diagnostic system, which has to allocate all cases presented into one of two mutually exclusive categories: those who will be taken into care and those who will not. If social workers require a high standard of evidence of abuse before they act, then some children may suffer serious injury or die from the abuse they receive before they are taken into care. Alternatively, if children are taken into care as soon as abuse is suspected, there will be a larger proportion of children taken into care who were not at risk, with consequent public concern. Wherever the threshold is set, there will be some incorrect attributions.

Principles of Signal Detection Theory

For consistency with the language of signal detection theory, the term 'positive' is generally used to denote the situation where the threshold has been exceeded, irrespective of whether this has positive or negative connotations (Swets, 1988, p1285). Similarly, the term 'negative' is used to denote a situation where the threshold is not reached. If the number of false and true attributions are expressed as a proportion of the true positives, then these proportions will sum to 1, as will the false and true attributions of true negatives. The behaviour of the system can then be described by two indices: the proportion of correctly attributed positives (called 'hits') and falsely attributed negatives ('false alarms') are usually chosen, although Sperling and Dosher (1986), argue that the use of hits and correct negatives gives more easily interpreted results.

This use of proportions satisfies the first of two properties required by Swets of a measure of the performance of a diagnostic system: that the measure should be unaffected by the proportion of positives and negatives in the test sample.

The second of Swets' requirements is that a measure of the performance of the system as a whole should be independent of the way that the decision criterion is set. In our example, we should want our measure of the accuracy of the diagnostic *system* to be the same whether the social workers are told to 'take no chances' and to take into care any children who appear to be at risk (a lenient criterion), or, alternatively, whether they are told to insist on a very high standard of proof before taking action (a strict criterion). The essence of signal detection theory is that the decision-consistency of the system is measured *over a wide range of operating conditions.*

In the following sections, signal detection theory is applied to two questions in National Curriculum Assessment. These have been chosen primarily because they illustrate two very different uses of SDT, and suitable data to show the use of SDT are already available.

Question 1: how hard should a statement of attainment be?

The Level to which a statement of attainment is allocated is fixed in law. However, since none of the statements of attainment are written precisely enough to provide an unambiguous meaning, then there is considerable flexibility in the calibration of the meaning of each statement. Indeed, since approximately 100 000 copies of each of the ten subject documents are in circulation, such calibration can be used as a way of 'making the National Curriculum make sense'. The question is where, within a Level should the statement be pitched?

If the item is pitched at a relatively easy Level, then a high proportion of those whose 'true Level' is the same as the Level to which the statement is assigned will achieve the statement. Unfortunately, the chance of a student whose true Level is below the Level of the statement also attaining the statement may be unacceptably high. Conversely, pitching a statement (or, what amounts to the same thing, an item in a test or SAT) more demandingly ensures that it is only achieved by those whose true Level is at or above that associated with the statement, but may also deny the statement to those who should achieve it. Whatever threshold is set, there will be classification inconsistencies. SDT provides a rational basis for choosing the threshold.

The example below draws on the work of Knight (1993), who used statistical simulations to derive estimates of the probability of getting a particular Level overall, given different probabilities of achieving statements.

Knight's model assumed that each student has a 'true Level', and modelled the achievement of the student as a stochastic process. All statements at a particular Level are regarded as equally difficult, and the probability that a student of a given Level of attainment would achieve a statement at that Level is denoted as $p_{L|L}$.

It is, of course, also possible that a student would achieve a statement at the next higher Level, and the probability of this, for each statement, was denoted as $p_{L|L+1}$.

Using an aggregation rule that assumed that a student had to achieve two-thirds of the SoAs (or items) to achieve a Level (in this case 4 out of 6), the probability (as a percentage) that a student would actually achieve their true Level (L), one Level below this (L-1) or one Level above this (L+1) is given in Table 1. The values for $p_{L|L}$ and $p_{L|L+1}$ tabulated are representative of values found in the 1992 Key Stage 3 national mathematics pilot held in the summer of 1992.

Table 1: Percentage of students achieving below, at or above their 'true' Level

Value of $p_{L\|L}$	0.6	0.6	0.6	0.7	0.7	0.7	0.8	0.8	0.8
Value of $p_{L\|L+1}$	0.2	0.3	0.4	0.2	0.3	0.4	0.2	0.3	0.4
Level L-1(%)	46	46	46	26	26	26	10	10	10
Level L(%)	52	47	36	72	67	56	88	83	72
Level L+1(%)	2	7	18	2	7	18	2	7	18

Thesc data were then used to simulate the decision-consistency of classification at the Level 5-6 boundary, which is the planned median attainment for the 14-year-old cohort.

If we assume that equal numbers of students will be truly at Level 5 and Level 6, the data in Table 1 can be used to provide an estimate of the number of students mis-classified at the Level 5-6 boundary. The results of this simulation are shown in Table 2, for a nominal group of 10 000 students. Table 2 also shows the proportion of 'hits' (i.e. the proportion of students given Level 6 who were truly Level 6) and 'false-alarms' (i.e. the proportion of students given Level 6 who were truly Level 5). These are shown as raw proportions (rows 7 and 8), and also converted into *z*-scores (rows 9 and 10). The *z*-scores are simply the inverse values of the normal distribution function, i.e., the number of standard deviations above or below the mean corresponding to the area represented by the proportions of hits and false-alarms. The difference between the *z*-scores for hits and false alarms is the most commonly used index of the sensitivity of the system, *d' (see* Macmillan and Creelman, 1991, for a demonstration of the fact that this index is independent of the threshold setting, as required by Swets).

Table 2: Estimated numbers of 14-year-olds achieving each level, and associated statistics

Value of p_{LL}	0.6	0.6	0.6	0.7	0.7	0.7	0.8	0.8	0.8
Value of p_{LL+1}	0.2	0.3	0.4	0.2	0.3	0.4	0.2	0.3	0.4
True level 5 achieving level 5	4952	4832	4568	4952	4832	4568	4952	4832	4568
True level 6 achieving level 5	1104	1104	1104	624	624	624	240	240	240
True level 5 achieving level 6	48	168	432	48	168	432	48	168	432
True level 6 achieving level 6	3896	3896	3896	4376	4376	4376	4760	4760	4760
Proportion of 'hits' (H)	0.779	0.779	0.779	0.875	0.875	0.875	0.952	0.952	0.952
Proportion of 'false-alarms' (F)	0.001	0.003	0.086	0.001	0.003	0.086	0.001	0.003	0.086
$z(H)$	0.77	0.77	0.77	1.15	1.15	1.15	1.66	1.66	1.66
$z(F)$	-2.31	-1.82	-1.36	-2.31	-1.82	-1.36	-2.31	-1.82	-1.36
Sensitivity, d'	3.09	2.59	2.13	3.47	2.97	2.51	3.98	3.48	3.02

If, in raising $p_{L|L}$ from (say) 0.6 to 0.7, we discovered the we also raised $p_{L|L+1}$ from 0.2 to 0.3, we can see by looking at Table 2 that we will have *decreased* the sensitivity of the system (2.97<3.09). If we regarded all mis-classifications as equally ‘costly’, and all correct classifications as equally beneficial, then (0.6, 0.2) would be preferable to (0.7, 0.3) as a pair of values for ($p_{L|L}$, $p_{L|L+1}$). The effects of intermediate values of $p_{L|L}$ and $p_{L|L+1}$ can be estimated either by interpolating the values given in Table 2, or by repeating the simulations with other values, since, as is clear from Tables 1 and 2, the effects of $p_{L|L}$ and $p_{L|L+1}$ on *d*’ are independent of each other.

This example illustrates a single case, at a particular Level boundary, with a particular aggregation rule, but the method used is quite general. Once we know [illegible] we can use the signal detection index of [illegible] ıum values of $p_{L|L}$ and $p_{L|L+1}$, and therefore, [illegible] ıt should be pitched.

[illegible] ent should ‘holistic’ assessment

[illegible] ection theory’s index of sensitivity was used [illegible] parameters could be estimated. However, in [illegible] itivity of the system is difficult to influence. [illegible] itivity of the system is fixed, the performance [illegible] e improved by changing the setting of the

[illegible], an example from social work was described. [illegible] the diagnosis may be fixed, but those involved [illegible] control over whether they were more likely to give a positive or a negative diagnosis. In other words, raters can have a cautious bias (favouring negative responses) or a bias towards positive responses.

Unfortunately, while signal detection theory provides a single standard index of sensitivity (i.e. *d*’), there is no single ‘best’ index of bias – in different applications different indices of bias will be more appropriate – and a discussion of the three most commonly-occurring measures is given in Macmillan and Creelman (1991, pp33-48).

However, all the measures of bias have the property that bias is independent of sensitivity, and in looking at the leniency of raters, we are interested in the variation of bias for a fixed sensitivity.

Gill (1993) gives data on the performance of groups of student-teachers in assigning holistic national curriculum Levels to an open-ended practical problem solving task. Only seven groups of students were involved, and no attempt was made to determine the representativeness of the sample. Nevertheless, the data can be used to illustrate the application of SDT to the quality of assessments. The method used here is the same as used by Swets (1988) in his illustrative example for diagnosis of X-rays of lesions as malignant or benign, and is also treated in some detail in Macmillan and Creelman (1991, p61).

The assignment of Levels to tasks can be envisaged as a series of adept/non-adept attributions at each of the boundaries between Levels. The difficulty of making such judgements of course depends on whether the 'true' Level of the task (in this case, the consensus of expert judges) is close to the boundary in question. We should expect even novices to be quite confident in assigning a 'true' Level 7 response as being above the threshold between Level 2 and Level 3, but less confident at assessing the same task with respect to the Level 7-Level 8 boundary.

The attributions were rated according to one of four categories:

a) almost certainly above the threshold;

b) probably above the threshold;

c) probably below the threshold;

d) almost certainly below the threshold.

The results are shown in Table 3, where *H* and *F* are the *cumulative* proportions of 'hits' and 'false-alarms' and $z(H)$ and $z(F)$ are the corresponding normal deviates.

Table 3: Performance of groups of student raters on holistic grading task

Rating category	Above threshold	Below threshold	*H*	*F*	$z(H)$	$z(F)$
a	27	1	0.473	0.018	-0.07	-2.10
b	20	8	0.825	0.164	0.94	-0.98
c	9	19	0.982	0.509	2.10	0.02
d	1	27	1.000	1.000		
total	57	55				

Figure 2 shows a plot of the pairs of false-positive proportion (false alarms) versus true-positive proportions (hits). The various (H, F) pairs are shown with a best fitting curve (in this case a spline) called the ROC (originally 'receiver operating characteristic', but now often 'relative operating characteristic') of the system. The important feature of this curve is that although the curve corresponds to a single value of the sensitivity of the diagnosis, it describes the accuracy of the system over different settings of the criterion.

Figure 2: Empirical p-scale ROC curve for students assessing pieces of coursework

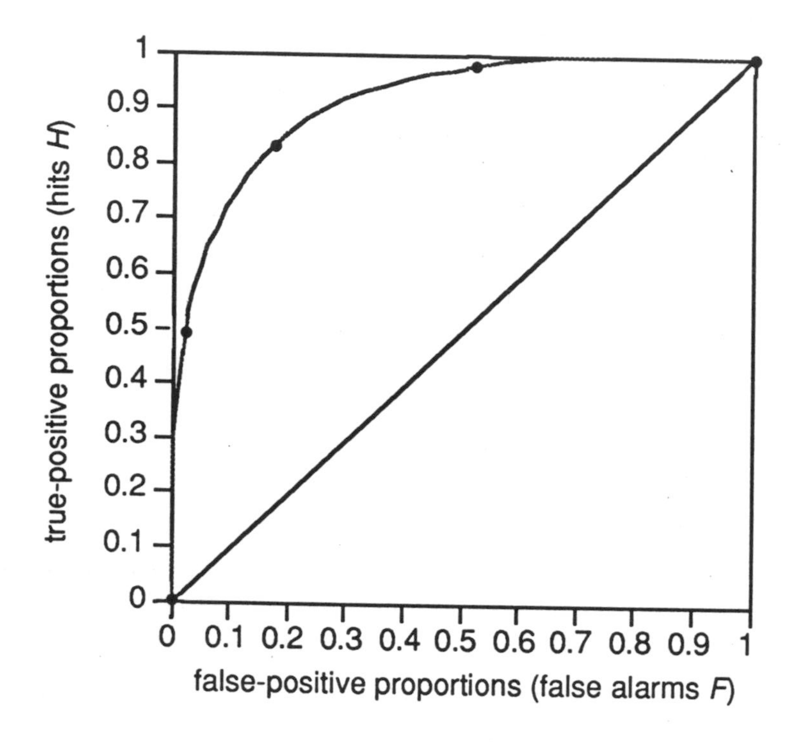

The fact that the value of *d'* represented by this ROC curve is reasonably constant is illustrated by the plot of the same data, after an inverse normal transformation (i.e. the $z(H)$ and $z(F)$ values given in the last two columns of Table 3) which is shown in figure 3.

If a single index, rather than a curve on a graph, is required, then Swets (1988, p1287) suggests that the area of the graph below the curve can be used as an index of decision consistency, which ranges from 0.50, when the ROC (i.e. Figure 2) is a diagonal line (corresponding to the situation where no discrimination exists) to 1.00 (where there are no incorrect classifications).

Figure 3: Empirical z-scale ROC curve for students assessing pieces of coursework

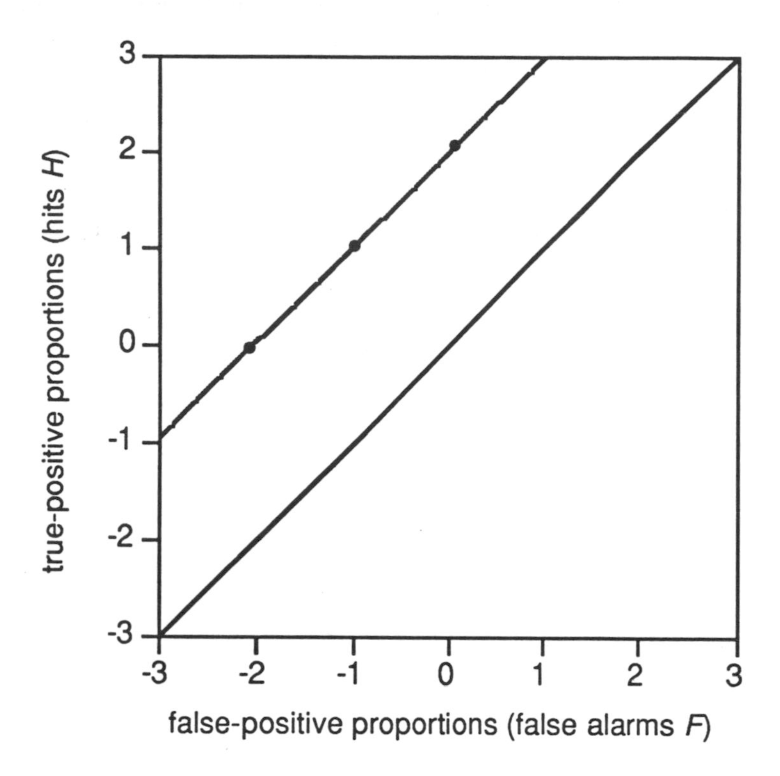

In fact there are a variety of ways of obtaining multiple (H, F) pairs to generate an ROC curve. Macmillan and Creelman (1991, pp 59-80) identify four such methods:

> *verbal instructions*: this method relies on the use of verbal instructions to the raters to vary their preparedness to say yes or no, so in the case of our social work example, separate runs (possibly with the same raters) would be conducted with different verbal instructions (i.e. 'be tough', 'don't take chances', etc.) .
>
> *monetary rewards*: the effect of verbal instructions can be intensified in certain cases by varying the monetary rewards paid to raters, so that we would expect much more positives when the relative benefit:cost payoff for hits and false alarms was 10:1 when compared with a ratio of (say) 1:10.
>
> *varying presentation probability*: in this method, the experiment is partitioned into several parallel experiments where the relative probabilities of the two outcomes (i.e. positive and negative) are different in each case.

rating scales: in this method raters are asked to make both a diagnosis, and asked to indicate the strength of their faith in their judgement. This can be done by offering the raters a four or six-point Likert-type scale, or by asking the raters first to make their diagnosis on a dichotomous basis, and then asked to indicate the strength of their faith in their judgement, typically on a three-point scale (Reber, Kassin, Lewis, and Cantor, 1980).

The principals of signal detection theory can also be combined with utility theory, in order to find the *optimum* setting of the criterion, taking into account the prior probabilities of the prevailing conditions, the costs of incorrect decision and the benefits of incorrect decisions.

If P_{pos} and P_{neg} are the prior probabilities, B_{TP} and B_{TN} are the benefits of true positives and true negatives respectively, and C_{FP} and C_{FN} are the costs associated with false positive and false negatives respectively, then the optimum slope of the ROC graph, S_{opt} is given (Swets, 1992 p525) by:

$$S_{opt} = \frac{P_{neg}}{P_{pos}} \times \frac{B_{TN} - C_{FP}}{B_{TP} - C_{FN}} \quad (3)$$

Since the slope of an ROC decreases strictly monotonically from left to right, the value of the slope determines uniquely the proportion of true positives and false positives that represent the optimum threshold, and these values can be read from the ROC graph.

Conclusion

Although in its infancy as a means for determining the accuracy of an assessment system, signal detection theory appears to hold considerable promise where essentially continuous data (e.g. the extent to which a student has achieved the attainments defined in a domain) has to be reported in a dichotomous way. It also allows a more rational approach to the setting of the cut score: the threshold between adept and non-adept.

However, it also has a major problem. This is that the sampling distribution of the index proposed by Swets (i.e. the area under the ROC curve) is not known, so that it is not possible to know to what extent ROC curves are significantly different from each other, or from the zero discrimination case (a diagonal straight line).

Despite this, it seems that signal detection theory offers significant scope within National Curriculum Assessment both as an informative and easily accessible measure of the accuracy of the assessment system, and also as a means of setting decision thresholds.

References

ACKERMAN, T. A. (1991). 'A didactic explanation of item bias, item impact and item validity from a multidimensional perspective', *Journal of Educational Measurement*, **29**, 1, 67-91.

AIRASIAN, P. (1987). 'State mandated testing and educational reform: context and consequences', *American Journal of Education*, **95**, 3, 393-412.

AIRASIAN, P. (1988). 'Measurement-driven instruction: a closer look', *Educational Measurement: Issues and Practice (Winter)*, 6-11.

AMERICAN PSYCHOLOGICAL ASSOCIATION, AMERICAN EDUCATIONAL RESEARCH ASSOCIATION, and NATIONAL COUNCIL ON MEASUREMENT USED IN EDUCATION (1954). 'Technical recommendations for psychological tests and diagnostic techniques', *Psychological Bulletin Supplement*, **51**, 2 part 2, whole issue (1-38).

ANASTASI, A. (1990). *Psychological Testing* (6 edn.). New York: Macmillan.

ANGOFF, W. H. (1988). 'Validity: an evolving concept'. In: WAINER, H. and BRAUN, H. I. (Eds.), *Test Validity* (pp. 19-32). Hillsdale, NJ: Lawrence Erlbaum Associates.

BECHTOLDT, H. P. (1959). 'Construct validity: a critique', *American Psychologist*, **14**, 619-629.

BROWN, F. (1980). 'Perspectives on validity', *NCME Measurement News*, **23**, 3-4.

COHEN, J. (1960). 'A coefficient of agreement for nominal scales', *Educational and Psychological Measurement*, **20**, 37-46.

CRONBACH, L. J. (1947). 'Test "reliability": its meaning and determination', *Psychometrika*, ***12***, 1, 1-16.

CRONBACH, L. J. (1971). 'Test validation'. In: THORNDIKE, R. L. (Ed.), *Educational Measurement* (pp. 443-507). Washington DC: American Council on Education.

CRONBACH, L. J., GLESER, G. C., NANDA, H., and RAJARATNAM, N. (1972). *The Dependability of Behavioural Measurements: Theory of Generalizability for Scores and Profiles*. New York, NY: Wiley.

CRONBACH, L. J., and MEEHL, P. E. (1955). 'Construct validity in psychological tests', *Psychological Bulletin*, **52**, 4, 281-302.

CRONBACH, L. J., RAJARATNAM, N., and GLESER, G. C. (1963). 'Theory of generalizability: a liberalization of reliability theory', *British Journal of Statistical Psychology,* **16**, 2, 137-163.

EMBRETSON (WHITELY), S. E. (1983). 'Construct validity - construct representation versus nomothetic span', *Psychological Bulletin,* **93**, 1, 179-197.

EMBRETSON, S. E. (1992). 'Psychometric models for learning and cognitive processes'. In: FREDERIKSEN, N., MISLEVY,R. J. and BEJAR I. (Eds.), *Test Theory for a New Generation of Tests* (pp. 125-150). Hillsdale, NJ: Lawrence Erlbaum Associates.

FELDT, L. S., and BRENNAN, R. L. (1989). 'Reliability'. In: LINN R. L. (Ed.), *Educational Measurement* (pp. 105-146). Washington, DC: American Council on Education/Macmillan.

GARRETT, H. E. (1937). *Statistics in Psychology and Education.* New York, NY: Longmans, Green.

GILL, P. N. G. (1993). 'Using the construct of "levelness" in assessing open work in the National Curriculum', *British Journal of Curriculum and Assessment,* **3**, 3, 17-18.

GOLDMAN, A. I. (1976). 'Discrimination and perceptual knowledge', *Journal of Philosophy,* **LXXIII**, 20, 771-791.

GREEN, D. M., and SWETS, J. A. (1966). *Signal Detection Theory and Psychophysics*. New York, NY: Wiley.

GRIFFITHS, A. P. (Ed.) (1967). *Knowledge and Belief.* Oxford, UK: Oxford University Press.

KITCHER, P. (1984). *The Nature of Mathematical Knowledge.* New York, NY: Oxford University Press.

Klein, P. D. (1971). 'A proposed definition of propositional knowledge', *Journal of Philosophy,* **LXVIII**, 16, 471-482.

KNIGHT, B. (1993) *'Theoretical and practical approaches to evaluating the reliability and dependability of national curriculum test outcomes'*. Paper presented at SEAC technical meeting on reliability in National Curriculum Assessment held at School Examinations and Assessment Council on 6.1.93.

LEHRER, K., and PAXSON, T. (1969). Knowledge: undefeated, justified, true belief. *Journal of Philosophy, LXV1*(8), 225-237.

LOEVINGER, J. (1947). 'A systematic approach to the construction and evaluation of tests of ability', *Psychological Monographs*, **61**, 4 (No. 285).

LOEVINGER, J. (1957). 'Objective tests as instruments of psychological theory', *Psychological Reports*, **3** (Monograph Supplement 9), 635-694.

MACMILLAN, N. A., and CREELMAN, C. D. (1991). *Signal Detection: a User's Guide*. Cambridge, UK: Cambridge University Press.

MESSICK, S. (1980). 'Test validity and the ethics of assessment', *American Psychologist*, **35**, 11, 1012-1027.

NUTTALL, D. L. (1987). 'The validity of assessments', *European Journal of Psychology of Education*, **2**, 2, 109-118.

POPHAM, W. J. (1978). *Criterion-referenced Measurement*. Englewood Cliffs, NJ: Prentice-Hall.

POPHAM, W. J. (1981). *Modern Educational Measurement*. Englewood Cliffs, NJ: Prentice Hall.

POPHAM, W. J., and HUSEK, T. R. (1969). 'Implications of criterion referenced measurement', *Journal of Educational Measurement*, **6**, 1, 1-9.

POPPER, K. R. (1963). *Conjectures and Refutations : the Growth of Scientific Knowledge*. London : UK: Routledge and Kegan Paul.

REBER, A. S., KASSIN, S. M., LEWIS, S., and CANTOR, G. W. (1980). 'On the relationship between implicit and explicit modes in the learning of a complex rule structure', *Journal of Experimental Psychology: Human Learning and Memory*, **92**, 81-110.

SEDDON, G. M. (1988). 'The validity of reliability measures', *British Educational Research Journal*, **14**, 1, 89-97.

SHANNON, C., and WEAVER, W. (1949). *The Mathematical Theory of Communication*. Urbana, IL: University of Illinois Press.

SPERLING, G., and DOSHER, B. A. (1986). 'Strategies and optimization in human information processing'. In: BOFF, K., THOMAS J., and KAUFMANN, L. (Eds.), *Handbook of Perception and Performance* New York, NY: Wiley.

SUBKOVIAK, M. J. (1980). 'Decision-consistency approaches'. In: R. A. BERK, R.A. (Ed.), *Criterion-referenced Measurement: the State of the Art* (pp. 129-185). Baltimore, MD: Johns Hopkins University Press.

SWETS, J. A. (1988). 'Measuring the accuracy of diagnostic systems', *Science*, **240**, 4857, 1285-1293.

SWETS, J. A. (1992). 'The science of choosing the right decision threshold in high-stakes diagnostics', *American Psychologist*, **47**, 4, 522-532.

TYLER, R. (1934). *Constructing Achievement Tests*. Columbus, OH: Ohio State University.

UNGER, P. (1968). 'An analysis of factual knowledge', *Journal of Philosophy*, **LXV**, 6, 157-170.

WILIAM, D. (1992) 'Technical issues in criterion-referenced assessment: evidential and consequential bases'. Paper presented at 18th Annual International Conference of the International Association for Educational Assessment held at St Patrick's College, Dublin, Eire.

WILIAM, D. (1993). 'Validity, dependability and reliability in National Curriculum Assessment', *The Curriculum Journal*, **4**, 4, 335-350.

WOOD, R. (1985). *Testing*. Milton Keynes, UK: Open University Press.

CHAPTER 3

THE RELIABILITY OF NATIONAL CURRICULUM ASSESSMENT AT KEY STAGES 1 AND 2

Diane Shorrocks and **Nick Nelson**
School of Education, University of Leeds

The group working in the School of Education, the University of Leeds has been involved with National Curriculum Assessment in several ways over the last three years. We carried out the formal, national evaluation of the first full run of the 1991 Key Stage 1 assessments (Shorrocks *et al.*, 1992), followed by a further, smaller evaluation of the 1992 assessments at this key stage (Shorrocks *et al.*,1993). We are currently developing the assessment materials in mathematics for Key Stage 2.

These experiences have provided us not only with a great deal of relevant material but also much food for thought on the matter of estimating the reliability of the NC assessments. This chapter will therefore have two major sections within it: an outlining of the central points raised by the two evaluations of the Key Stage 1 assessments followed by further issues raised by the present test development process for Key Stage 2 mathematics: this chapter therefore embodies both retrospect and prospect.

Reliability in the Key Stage 1 assessments: the ENCA 1 Project

This project, funded by SEAC, had a broad specification, as listed below. The evaluation was to carry out in-depth assessment of a national sample of children, to provide evidence from which it would be possible to:

- compare the National Curriculum Assessment results with those obtained from the in-depth studies;
- consider the range of achievements of individuals and groups in different assessment tasks;
- highlight aspects of National Curriculum Assessment that could be improved by modifications to SAT and TA procedures;
- explore the validity and reliability of attainment level scores as indicators of progression;

- investigate the results of combining SAT and TA information and the validity of the single scores derived;
- explore the stability of National Curriculum Assessment results across different groups of pupils.

These specifications in themselves raised questions, not least in the terminology employed. What was also clear was that the focus of the specification was on the **products** of assessments and not on the **process**. These points were discussed and the final evaluation had both a process and a product focus. The term 'reliability' was questioned, in the light of the criterion-referenced nature of the National Curriculum assessments. In the context of the present chapter, four key issues will now be addressed, before moving on to the substance of some of the findings on the reliability of the outcomes.

Criterion-referenced assessment, emerging in the 1960s as a reaction against norm-referenced approaches that seemed to offer little help to educators concerned with the direct issue of learning and teaching, is an idea that itself needs clarification. In the extensive American (eg Glaser, 1963; Popham, 1980) literature on the topic, a wide range of terms are encountered: criterion-referenced; domain-referenced; objectives-referenced; competency-based testing; mastery testing. In the British literature, more recent and more limited in scope, the term 'criterion-referenced assessment' has often been used, applying to a range of approaches that are not overtly norm-referenced.

The central question is one of determining the purpose of the assessment: what is the assessment for? If the purpose of the assessment is to make relative judgements, then it will be described as norm-referenced: if the purpose is to make judgements against a more absolute standard of some kind, then it will be described as criterion-referenced. The precise kind of criterion-referencing will depend on the comparison being made, the reasons for making the comparison, and the nature of the standard or criterion being used. This implies at least two clear aspects of definition, namely the question of domain definition and mastery definition.

The domains addressed by an assessment need to be clearly defined and understood, a principle that is easily stated but difficult to implement, for reasons that are well rehearsed in the arena of educational objectives (Black and Dockrell, 1984). Domains vary in their amenability to definition, their open or more closed character and their homogeneity or heterogeneity. Neither is the question of mastery definition an easy one. Since domains vary in the ways just outlined, decisions about mastery of that domain will also vary. If all the elements in a domain are known and specified, the domain can be sampled in ways that reflect this appropriately: where the domain is not specified, or even specifiable, in this way, then the question of mastery levels becomes highly problematic.

As this chapter will go on to show, the National Curriculum, as presently conceived, represents a set of specifications and criteria that are hugely varied and in many cases ambiguous. Even the attempts at reworking in some of the subjects (e.g. mathematics and science) have not resolved this issue. Economy of scale has been achieved at the expense of criteria (the statements) that are either more tightly-packed in terms of content domains or more general and ambiguous. As such, the dependability of tests and assessments designed to measure performance against them, is brought into considerable question.

To compound this problem, the resulting assessment outcomes are specifiable in terms of only a limited number of categories, the ten levels, now under severe question as a measure of progression (Dearing, 1993). At the first two key stages this scale is effectively reduced to a six or seven category scale, Levels 1 to 6 with the further designation 'W' for children working towards Level 1. Scores are also progressively aggregated, a process in which detailed information is gradually lost, subsumed under a single, categoric score.

Traditional notions of reliability are therefore inappropriate in the context of National Curriculum assessments. Measures of reliability derived from a single test administration such as Alpha (Cronbach,1951) or the Kuder-Richardson formulae (Kuder and Richardson, 1937)) are principally concerned with the internal consistency of the scale. Internal consistency is a function of the dimensionality of the scale, although as McDonald (1981) points out the two terms are not equivalent because a scale either is or is not n-dimensional, but might have varying degrees of internal consistency. NCA scores are derived from heterogeneous collections of behaviours (SoAs) and as such it does not seem reasonable to assume that the scales would be either unidimensional or internally consistent.

Given these characteristics, the test and assessment outcomes in the National Curriculum can really only be seen as, at best, fairly gross characterisations of a child's knowledge, understanding and skills. A child is awarded a score in terms of Levels, which both within and between the subjects in the curriculum, show considerable variability in content, range and difficulty. It is not the most straightforward of frameworks within which to work, as the 1992 evaluation report emphasised (Shorrocks *et al.*,op. cit.). Under these circumstances, the issue of judging the reliability or dependability of the outcomes becomes translated into one of **decision consistency**. Is the Level a child is awarded by one or more of the assessments a 'true' grading, and an appropriate reflection of that child's knowledge and skills? To the extent that the assessment is a dependable one, then true positives and true negatives will be the result. To the extent that they are unreliable, then false positives and false negatives will occur, each with their own educational consequences. The aim must be to maximise the former and minimise the latter.

To return to the Key Stage 1 evaluations, the main work of the 1991 evaluation was to compare the results of NCA with those obtained from the in-depth re-assessment study of a national sample of children. Specially developed assessment materials were used and specially trained researchers (experienced primary teachers, heads, etc.), and comparing the results of these re-assessments with the teacher assessment scores they had been awarded and with the SAT scores they obtained.

Spelling this out even more clearly, an estimation of the reliability of the scoring outcomes on NCA was provided by investigation of the relationship between TA scores, SAT scores and what might be called 'ENCA scores', in the three core subjects (English, mathematics and science). Before discussing the statistical approach adopted, it is necessary to highlight the fact that three distinct sets of scores were being compared, each with somewhat different characteristics, and at a point in time when schools and teachers were inexperienced in such matters and not necessarily familiar with the detail of the National Curriculum in the core subjects. The scores were in principle comparable, since the same children were being assessed against the same criteria. However, they were not so clearly comparable in two important ways: the three kinds of assessment were not carried out by the same people (the children's class teachers carried out TA and administered the SATs but not the special assessments) and they were carried out at rather different points in time. These factors would inevitably influence the outcomes and comparisons, but should also provide the starting point for asking important questions about the relationships between the three and the wider educational and assessment implications.

The method chosen to compare the sets of scores was Cohen's **Kappa** (Cohen, 1960). The NC Levels are supposed to represent an ordinal scale and, given different measures in relation to them, could be compared using one of several techniques for measuring association (c^2 , Phi, etc.) but in these cases, there could be high levels of **association** in a predictive sense (particularly with a large sample) but not necessarily much **agreement** in the scores. As such, the scores would be difficult to interpret. Agreement could be determined by straightforward comparison of the proportion of a sample whose categorisation is identical, but Kappa takes into account the fact that a proportion of such agreements would occur by chance. This is particularly important where more than two measures are being compared. Kappa was chosen to be the summary statistic used for comparing the sets of equivalent ratings/Levels in NC. It essentially compares the amount of agreement actually found (the observed agreement) with the expected agreement, which is the amount of agreement that would occur if the sets of scores were independent.

Interpreting the significance of the values of Kappa that emerge from comparisons is not straightforward. If the observed agreement is equal to the expected agreement, then Kappa takes the value 0. If there is total agreement, then Kappa takes the value 1. A suggested set of benchmarks for values of Kappa in between has been provided by Landis and Koch (1977), although there is always an element of subjectivity in the judgement.

0.00	poor	0.41 - 0.60	moderate
0.01 - 0.20	slight	0.61 - 0.80	substantial
0.21 - 0.40	fair	0.81 - 1.00	almost perfect

Some of the results from the 1991 and 1992 evaluations

The ENCA and NUT reports (op. cit.) give full details of all the analyses and findings of the two projects. Only one or two sections of information will be presented and discussed here. Table 1 gives the values of Kappa for a selection of the Attainment Targets (old Orders in mathematics and science) when **TA** scores and **SAT** scores were compared in 1991 and 1992.

The significant points to emerge occurred both across attainment targets and across years. In the first year (1991), there were moderate levels of agreement (though no higher) in English, a subject where it might be considered teachers had most experience and confidence in assessment terms. There was much less agreement in the mathematics attainment targets, and in science, the agreement was poor to fair. By 1992, however, the values of Kappa in the English score comparisons increased considerably, reaching almost perfect agreement in some. In the mathematics and science scores, where the AT was included in both consecutive years, there was also a considerable increase in agreement: when the ATs were 'new' that year, however, the values of Kappa were once again somewhat lower. Throughout, the agreement in 1992 was higher than in 1991. Further analysis of the scores indicated that teacher assessment scores were higher in 1991 than in 1992, bringing them closer into line with the SAT scores and accounting for much of the increased agreement and higher scores in 1992. The long-term implications of such changes in scoring outcomes warrant much closer investigation.

Table 1: Values of Kappa for selected attainment targets (English, mathematics and science) in the 1991 and 1992 scores (agreement between TA and SAT scores)

AT	1991 scores		1992 scores	
	Kappa	n	Kappa	n
En2	.59	2427	.88	1515
En3	.46	2507	.76	1516
En4	.49	2505	.85	1522
En5	.58	2405	.90	1516
Ma1	.34	2510		
Ma3	.36	2497	.76	1520
Ma5	.29	808		
Ma8	.43	154		
Ma10	.25	1242		
Ma12			.65	879
Ma13	.48	343		
Ma14			.45	751
Sc1	.27	2508		
Sc3	.23	1959		
Sc5	.00	78*		
Sc6	.24	54*	.69	1003
Sc9			.44	644

Note: * indicates a small number of cases in ATs where there was choice

When the ENCA scores were included in these comparisons, a rather varied pattern of results occurred. The ENCA assessments were very detailed, with all SoA and all attributes within the SoA being assessed, unlike the SAT. To render the scores more directly comparable, the mastery criteria used in the SAT were replicated from within the total ENCA scores, i.e. a sub-set of the scores was used that matched the SAT, in so far as the detail of the performance criteria set out in the SAT allowed it. The overriding finding was that the ENCA scores were mostly lower than the SAT scores and frequently lower than the TA scores. This is an interesting finding that deserves even more investigation than could be given in the final report of the Project. It potentially provides interesting information on the effects of different kinds of assessment approach at different levels of detail.

There was poor agreement between TA and ENCA scores and between SAT and ENCA scores. The only exception to this was Ma3, where the comparison with the SAT score gave a value of Kappa that reached .42 (moderate). The result of comparing both TA and SAT scores with in-depth, individualised assessments was to demonstrate very little agreement in the sets of outcomes. This is not to suggest that the ENCA scores were in any way the benchmark, or the 'gold standard' as it were. Rather, it is to show that, in the first year of the Key Stage 1 assessments at least, the dependability of the outcomes could be brought into considerable question.

One final point bears further illustration, concerning the use of Kappa as an index of agreement. In Sc14 (Sound and Music - old Orders) the following distributions of scores across the Levels were obtained for the TA scores and the ENCA scores, as shown in Table 2 below. Here, the distributions were almost identical (no significant difference), but the value of Kappa was close to zero: the same children had not been allocated to the same Levels although the overall outcomes were the same. Table 3 goes on to show the nature of the disagreements in terms of the percentage of pupils being awarded the Levels in the two sets of scores.

Table 2: Percentage agreement and value of Kappa for TA and ENCA distributions in Sc14

	Levels			
	W	1	2	3
TA scores	8	36	53	3
ENCA scores	5	34	56	5

n = 229

Percentage Agreement = 45%

Kappa = 0.06 (upper limit = 0.15, lower limit = -0.02)

Table 3: Percentage of different Levels awarded in the TA and ENCA scores for Sc14.

Differences in Levels awarded						
-3	-2	-1	0	+1	+2	+3
0%	4%	19%	45%	27%	5%	0%

Some general issues and principles

In curriculum assessment, it seems important to be able to estimate the dependability of the assessment based on one administration. First, there is a need to decide exactly what measure (or measures) are implicated in this estimation of dependability. At present, the intended outcome of the assessment process is the classification of each child into one of a discrete number of Levels for each of the attainment targets separately, and subsequently for the mathematics curriculum overall. This suggests that we should be looking for some measure of classification consistency with respect to the allocation of children to Levels within an AT. This allocation is made by applying certain arbitrary, but precisely defined aggregation rules to the results for each statement of attainment. Because the aggregation process is based on defined rules, the probability of a consistent final classification depends solely on, and may be calculated from, the probability of consistent decisions with respect to each of the SoA involved in the aggregation.

For example, we may consider the situation where a Level with three SoAs is assessed on two occasions. For each of the SoAs there are three possibilities. The child may achieve the SoA on both occasions, not achieve on both occasions, or achieve the SoA on one occasion but not the other. This last possibility would be regarded as an inconsistency. If we know the probabilities of the child achieving on the two occasions, and we assumed that achievement on the two occasions was independent, then it follows that the probabilities of the three kinds of outcome for the SoAs are :

outcome	**probability**
achieves twice	PaPb
fails twice	(1-Pa)(1-Pb)
achieves on the first occasion and fails on the second	Pa(1-Pb)
fails on the first occasion and achieves on the second	(1-Pa)Pb

where Pa and Pb are the probabilities of achievement on the two occasions

These equations may be combined to give the overall probabilities of consistent and inconsistent response patterns:

$$\text{probability of consistency} = 1 + 2PaPb - Pa - Pb$$

$$\text{probability of inconsistency} = Pa + Pb - 2PaPb$$

It is not difficult to show that a high expectation of classification consistency is only obtained when the probabilities of attainment on the two occasions are both close to 1 or both close to 0. Similarly, a low expectation of consistency arises when the probabilities of achievement are low on one occasion and high on the other.

If the probability of an inconsistent classification is known for each statement of attainment, then the likely outcome in terms of Level can be calculated. With three SoAs and using the 'n-1' aggregation rule, it follows that:

- If all three SoAs are consistent, then the level is consistent
- If one SoA is inconsistent, then the level is consistent if the other two SoA are both achieved or both failed.
- If two SoAs are inconsistent, then the level is inconsistent if the inconsistencies are in the same direction
- If all three SoAs are inconsistent, then the award of the level is always inconsistent.

Using the above relations, it is possible to calculate the probability of an inconsistent Level classification using only the probabilities of the child achieving on the various items. The problem lies, of course, in determining what these probabilities are. The solution requires a model for attainment within each of the SoAs.

Modelling attainment is never straightforward, and there seem to be particular difficulties in the National Curriculum Assessment context. The criterion-relatedness of each item has to be maintained, even under a new regime of producing test scores based on a total aggregation of marks. In other words, an item is judged first on whether it fits a particular SoA or part of an SoA. This ties the development of items to the curriculum framework within which the assessment is constrained to operate. Unfortunately, the curriculum framework lacks coherence in the sense that each Level within an AT often consists of a number of structurally disparate behavioural domains (SoAs). It is possible that no model of attainment is appropriate for all domains, in which case there are two options open to us. On the one hand we could develop a variety of models each of which seem to work for different kinds of domain; alternatively we could seek to restructure the curriculum framework itself.

Of the two options, the first seems, at present, to be the more feasible. In the mathematics curriculum, for example, there are domains in which the behaviour required is essentially recall of facts. These domains are generally well defined and often relatively unordered in character. In these circumstances, the most appropriate model would seem to be random sampling of the elements in the domain, and the appropriate metric for measuring attainment would be an estimate of the (universe) proportion correct score. If there is no correlation between the child's knowledge of the individual facts, and the domain completely unordered, then the probability of a child achieving an assessment item based on one such fact will be the same as the child's true proportion correct score. Such a success will also be independent of success or failure on any other such item. In these circumstances, dependable estimation of each child's domain score requires a fairly large number of items.

On the other hand, there are mathematical behaviours which are essentially algorithmic in nature. In domains of this kind, modelling attainment in terms of internally consistent items conforming to scale of progression or developmental trait may be appropriate. If, for such a domain, it could be demonstrated that there was a perfect hierarchy for all possible items, then a single item selected at some arbitrary level of difficulty would dependably separate the children into those who can achieve at that level or above and those who cannot.

In reality it is unlikely that any of the assessment domains derived from SoAs in the mathematics curriculum will be found to conform to either of these extremes; models of attainment which fit real-world SoAs need to be developed. It is hoped that investigation of the structure of the SoAs, and of the relationships between the cognitive demands of the elements within them will produce models of attainment which fit real data.

In National Curriculum Assessment, as with all assessment and testing regimes, it is generally true that the more items there are, the more dependable will be the final classification. Unfortunately, the more items there are in a National Curriculum Assessment package, the less 'manageable' it is deemed to be. At the moment, manageability seems to be taking precedence in determining the appropriate number of items for an assessment package.

Because the overall number of items in the assessment package is severely constrained by the 'manageability' issue, we need to be careful how we allocate them. It may be that the internal structure of some SoAs means that they can be assessed using proportionately fewer items than would be required to assess other SoAs at the same level of dependability.

Conclusions

The overriding conclusion reached in the evaluation of the 1991 Key Stage 1 assessments was that the reliability, or more appropriately, the dependability of the scoring outcomes left a great deal to be desired. Much of this was the result of the inexperience of teachers putting such a system in place for the first time, combined with a training programme that was characterised by enormous variability across schools and LEAs. The 1992 assessments seemed to have rectified some of these anomalies, at least in terms of the amount of agreement found between the sets of scores derived fron the SATs and those based on teacher assessment.

It has often been said that one of the purposes of the SATs was that of calibration: experience of administering the SATs should provide clearer guidance to teachers as to the implied interpretations of the SoAs and the mastery levels required. In some senses, this has clearly occurred, but of course, it begs the question as to whether the two sets of outcomes **should** be similar.

This has been a problematic issue from the inception of the whole system, and one that is currently being addressed in the major review that is taking place. The present strategy seems to favour a more distinct separation between the wide-ranging assessments made by the teacher, which may be both formative and summative in purpose and character, and the kinds of assessments provided by one-off, pencil and paper tests as in the SATs. This will clarify some of the present difficulties, but at a cost. Only in so far as the short tests embody and overtly exemplfy an interpretation of the SoAs, can they continue to act in a calibrating and moderating kind of way. A valid, reliable and dependable assessment system, particulary in the earlier key stages, still seems some way off.

References

BLACK, H. D,. and DOCKRELL, W. B.(1984). *Criterion Referenced Assessment in the Classroom. Edinburgh:* Scottish Council for Research in Education.

COHEN, S.(1960). 'A coefficient of agreement for nominal scales', *Educational and Psychological Measurement*, **20**.

CRONBACH, L. S. (1951). 'Coefficient Alpha and the internal structure of tests', *Psychometrica*, **16**.

DEARING, R. (1993). *The National Curriculum and its Assessment: Interim Report* . London: NCC and SEAC.

GLASER, R. (1963). 'Instructional technology and the measurement of learning outcomes', *American Psychologist*, **18**.

KUDER, G. F. and RICHARDSON, M. W. (1937). 'The theory and estimation of test reliability', *Psychometrica*, **2**.

LANDIS, J.R., & KOCH, G.G.,(1977) *'The measurement of observer agreement for categorical data', Biometrics*, **36**.

McDONALD, R. P. (1981). 'The dimensionality of tests and items', *British Journal of Mathematical and Statistical Psychology*, **34**.

POPHAM, W. J. (1980). 'Domain specification strategies.' In: BERK, R. A.(Ed.) *Criterion Referenced Measurement*. London: Johns Hopkins Press.

SHORROCKS ,D., DANIELS, S., FROBISHER, L., NELSON, N., WATERSON, A. and BELL, J. (1992). *The Evaluation of National Curriculum Assessment at Key Stage 1. Final Report of the ENCA 1 Project*. London: School Examinations and Assessment Council.

SHORROCKS, D., DANIELS, S., STAINTON, R.and RING, K. (1993). *Assessing Six- and Seven-year-olds at Key Stage 1. A report on the 1992 Key Stage 1 Assessments*. London: National Union of Teachers.

CHAPTER 4

TEACHER ASSESSMENT: A SOCIOLOGICAL PERSPECTIVE

Ann Filer, University of the West of England

Abstract

The advent of the Education Reform Act entailed the introduction into schools in England and Wales of two new forms of assessment, standard assessment tasks and teacher assessment. Despite its mistrust of teacher assessment, the Conservative Government has consistently made claims for the objectivity and comparability of this form of assessment as an achievable aim. There exists, however, within the literature of the sociology of assessment, a body of knowledge which, though developed pre-National Curriculum, represents a challenge to such claims. This paper reviews the predominant themes in that literature. In addition, it outlines some elements of a recent longitudinal ethnography in a primary school with respect to the way in which pedagogies can be analysed for the purposes of developing these traditional themes in the context of current assessment concerns. The sample consisted of a cohort of some 26 white working-class children passing through Years 1 to 3 of a primary school in the south of England.

Policy issues

National assessment in England and Wales

The arguments in this paper are grounded in and evolved out of the provision for assessment related to the National Curriculum for England and Wales (Department of Education and Science [DES], 1988).

In the implementation of the 1988 Education Reform Act, schools are required to record each pupil's performance against statements of attainment in the interests of identifying strengths and weaknesses and planning the progress of individuals through National Curriculum attainment targets. They are, in addition, required to bring together the results of teacher assessments and the results of standard assessments tasks at the end of three key stages when pupils are aged 7, 11 and 14. These summative results are intended to provide parents, schools, LEAs and the Government with clear and comparable information about the achievements of pupils and schools (DES, 1989a). Teacher assessment in the context of the National Curriculum thus has three main concerns. It is about monitoring and making informed decisions about progress of pupils on a day-to-day basis. It is concerned with the continuity of children's progress as they move from teacher to teacher and from school to school. It is, in addition, concerned with making comparisons between results emanating from individual classes, schools and LEAs.

It is generally recognised that Conservative governments since 1988 have had little faith in the reliability of teacher assessment compared with the supposed reliability and validity of national standardised tests. Whilst this is so, teacher assessments and reporting nevertheless help to underpin and lend legitimacy to the government's notion of parental choice of schools in an educational market place. It is therefore vital from the government's point of view that the message goes out that reliability can be achieved. Comparisons of the achievements of both individual schools and of individual pupils are to be made and the limited scope of SATs means that they cannot bear the weight of those comparisons alone. In the light of this consideration it is perhaps not surprising that one of the current rhetorics of education promulgated by Her Majesty's Inspectorate (HMI), the School Examinations and Assessment Council (SEAC), local education authorities and the educational press has been concerned with the possibility of 'objective' and 'systematic' teacher assessments as a realistic goal. Objectivity in teacher assessment can be achieved, it has been claimed, by the improvement of teachers' skills of observing and assessing and reaching comparability of understanding between teachers and schools of the implications of various statements of attainment against which pupils are measured (SEAC 1989; DES 1989a, 1989b, 1991). Much effort has been put into systematising teachers' skills and understandings in this way. Primary teachers have been encouraged to take a professional pride in the development of these skills, and the message that has gone out is that teachers are 'getting there' (DES, 1991; Alexander *et al.*, 1992, Hofkins, 1991, 1992). The second claim to 'objectivity' lies in the fact that no statement is to be made about pupils' underlying ability or effort etc., but that recognition shall be given only to observable behaviour for which evidence exists (SEAC, 1989).

The push for more refinement of teachers' assessment skills continues despite, or perhaps because of, overwhelming evidence of the poor comparability of results across different contexts of assessment. Recent studies, as well as showing problems with validity and reliability of SAT testing, also show that in many instances there is a poor correlation between SAT scores and teacher assessment (SEAC, 1991; Shorrocks, *et al.*, 1992; Abbott *et al.*, 1994). The Evaluation of National Curriculum Assessment (ENCA, Shorrocks *et al.*, 1992) carried out on behalf of SEAC showed a poor correlation between SATs, teacher assessment and independent assessments of statements of attainment. ENCA reported that, in their study of 2,440 children across three assessment contexts, 'the scoring outcomes left something to be desired in terms of dependability, validity and comparability'.

This lack of agreement of scores should not surprise us. Broadfoot *et al.*, (1991) cite Black (1990) in pointing out that: '...the mode of assessment used has direct implications for performance with identical tasks presented in different ways producing varied results' (Broadfoot *et al.*, 1991).

Two discourses of assessment

Kress (drawing on Foucault, 1971, 1980; Voloshinov, 1973) uses the term discourse in a specific way to denote something akin to genre or 'a way of talking on a given matter' (Kress, 1985,:144). The above concerns of DES, SEAC and HMI for improving teachers' skills in assessing are concerns regarding the achievement of objectivity and comparability of assessments through increased reliability and validity. In this the Government has placed the arguments concerning objectivity within a discourse that is concerned with the technology of assessment. A discourse of the technology of assessment is one in which required ends – in this case comparisons of classroom assessment results – are not in dispute. It is a discourse about the means whereby such ends can be achieved as fairly and objectively as possible. The Government's use of a technological discourse with respect to national assessment is, therefore, about the legitimation of assessment results and, by extension, of the uses to which they are put.

There is, though, an alternative discourse of assessment. This discourse gives us some insight into the fact that the assessments that teachers make of their pupils have origins in a field of activity that is invisible within the above discourse. It is a discourse in which assessment can be seen in terms of social processes, and assessment results can be seen as a product of that process. In this paper, I present a review of the literature of the sociology of assessment from this perspective. In addition I give an account of a recent research study which develops some of the major themes from past works within the context of national assessment in a primary school. The paper raises important questions concerning the limitations of what one can legitimately do with the assessments which varying classroom contexts give rise to.

Theoretical issues: assessment as social activity

Formal assessments now being made in primary schools certainly have the **appearance** of being more objective than they did pre-National Curriculum. Records, often in the form of ticked boxes, based on observations with 'evidence' to back them up and carefully worded reports to parents are now replacing the 'frequently generalised, laconic statements' (Alexander *et al.*, 1992) that parents and subsequent teachers have traditionally received. There is though, in the current drive for 'objective' assessment, a disregard for the message which historically has emanated from sociological study of the processes of classroom assessment. Consistently, this literature has pointed to the importance of viewing such assessments, both formal and informal, with some tentativeness. Such studies show that in evaluating pupils' academic skills, teachers inevitably include a measure of other attributes and dispositions. Mehan (1973) described assessments made by teachers of their pupils as 'interpretive, interactional accomplishments'. Teacher expectations, children's performance on earlier questions, reports from other teachers, all influenced decisions about the correctness of children's responses. Many other studies show that teachers, to varying degrees, make informal evaluations of children based on dispositional attributes which influence their evaluations of pupils' academic abilities. The mixing of dispositional, often social class-based attributes, with academic attributes has been observed to influence teacher decisions, for example on streaming and on lesson content, across the age range from nursery education through to secondary school (e.g. Rist, 1970; Douglas, 1964; Keddie, 1971).

The Government concerns for objectivity and comparability of assessment go some way towards addressing these issues. Problems of interpretations and expectations may, as outlined above, be reduced by the Government concerns for raising teachers' awareness of them and by honing their skills in assessing and by gathering 'evidence'. However, from the point of view of a discourse of assessment as social process, this is to take a limited and simplistic view of the problem of achieving objectivity. Within this discourse it has been shown that subjective and erroneous evaluations of pupils' abilities that teachers make, often informally, can go on to produce a reality that reflects those original evaluations. The work of Rist (1970) and Douglas (1964), cited above, and many others (Jackson, 1964; Rosenthal and Jacobsen 1968; Sharp and Green, 1975; Nash, 1976) suggested strongly that the cause of some of the academically differentiated outcomes for children lay in the working out of self-fulfilling prophesies in the classroom. This was particularly shown to be so with respect to differentiation by social class. Differences in the allocation of social as well as academic tasks to different groups of pupils, different uses of praise and control strategies, as well as different degrees of warmth towards different groups, have all been implicated in this process (Rist, 1970; Good and Brophy, 1970; Silberman, 1969). Differing treatments which children receive have been shown to result in social and learning outcomes which fulfil teachers' initial expectations. Similar studies have been made showing how differences in educational outcomes originated in stereotypical expectations made on the basis of race (Eggleston, 1988; Mortimore *et al.*, 1988) and gender (Cheshire and Jenkins, 1990, 1991; Walden and Walkerdine, 1985; Licht and Dweck, 1984).

Thus formal, 'objective' assessments can be products of earlier informal, subjective assessments and the processes that those earlier assessments set in motion.

Many of the subjective assessments which give rise to differing treatments and differing outcomes for pupils, have been seen in terms of thc 'typifications' which teachers make of pupils as a means by which they handle the complex social environment of the classroom. These typifications become part of teachers' commonsense classroom knowledge and will be favourable or unfavourable according to the extent to which qualities in pupils enable teachers to cope and to which pupils are rewarding to teach. The content of typification is grounded in the complex interaction of teacher biography, teaching styles, cultural influences and expectations of the institutional settings in which teachers find themselves (Becker, 1952; Hargreaves, 1978; Leiter, 1974; Pollard, 1985; Zeichner, *et al.*, 1987).

A discourse of assessment as social process, therefore, sees assessment, not merely as an activity in which expectations and interpretations can blur teacher observations. It sees assessment in addition as:

1. a product of a teacher-created context;
2. having a role in classroom differentiating processes;
3. a product of wider field of social action beyond the classroom.

In the past however, the literature concerned with assessment as a social activity has primarily been concerned with the nature of teacher judgements and assessment outcomes as they pertain to individuals and groups. Increasingly though, assessment results are being used to fulfil different purposes than has formerly been the case. With the introduction of the National Curriculum, assessments, as well as being used to monitor and compare the progress of individuals, are now being used for purposes of accountability of teachers and schools and to make comparisons between their 'performances'. Research into the processes of assessment accordingly, needs to shift its focus in order to examine objectivity of assessments for a class and for comparability of classes as well as for individuals. For such purposes, it needs to move away from a study of one-to-one, teacher-pupil perceptions and interactions and take a more holistic view of the classroom processes involved in pupil assessment. In so doing, this study explores and develops the above themes of the role of assessment in a differentiating process, as a product of a teacher-created classroom context and as product of a wider field of action beyond the classroom. To this end, classroom contexts and the pedagogies which give rise to them are analysed in terms of 'coping strategies' and in terms of 'the framing of educational knowledge'.

Analysing contexts of assessment

Coping strategies

Coping strategies constitute the broad base of classroom policy which teachers construct in the management of contradictory educational goals and ideologies and in response to a range of material and social constraints and opportunities (Hargreaves, 1978). They will necessarily cope in individualised ways according to a range of biographical, and socialising experiences from both within and beyond their professional experience (Pollard, 1985). The concept of coping strategies enables an analysis of classroom strategies in terms of both a range of organisational strategies and strategies for the control of pupils. A typology of teacher strategies in these respects can, Pollard suggests, be stated in terms of the strategies of 'routinization', 'manipulation', 'domination' and 'open negotiation' (Pollard, 1985).

The framing of educational knowledge

Bernstein (1971) refers to educational knowledge as being realised through the three message systems of curriculum, pedagogy and evaluation. 'Frame' in this context is used to determine the structure of the message system of pedagogy. It refers to the degree of control teacher and taught possess over selection, organisation and pacing of educational knowledge and to the strength of the boundary between what may or may not be transmitted in the pedagogic relationship as education knowledge. Bernstein points out that an important aspect of framing with respect to boundary maintenance concerns the degree to which teachers insulate educational knowledge from their own and their pupils' everyday knowledge. I do not differentiate, as Bernstein does, between educational knowledge and the everyday knowledge of teacher and taught in my analysis as this is not an altogether appropriate distinction for examining frame strength in an infant classroom. Rather, I differentiate between what I term 'curriculum knowledge', that is, what has been decided will be taught, and pupil perceptions, knowledge and interests.

In a longitudinal ethnography of teacher assessment in a primary school (Filer, 1993a, 1993b, 1993c), the analytical concepts of coping strategies and of the framing of educational knowledge were used to analyse the contexts in which teachers made a range of both formal (National Curriculum-related) and informal assessments of pupils. A cohort of children and their teachers was studied weekly through Years1,2, and 3 by means of participant observation. Data were also gathered from teacher and pupil interviews, documentary evidence in the form of school records and pupils' work, video and sound recordings.

The value of an analysis of the contexts of assessment in terms of 'coping' and 'framing' in developing the three themes was as follows.

A. *Assessment as a product of a teacher-created context.*
A focus on various organisational and control strategies as well as strategies for the control of knowledge in classrooms enabled an analysis of particular ways in which pupil responses were circumscribed by elements of the teaching context. This in turn enabled me to be specific about ways in which the assessments made were related to the contexts in which they were made; ie, were a product of those contexts.

B. *Assessment and differentiating processes in classrooms.*
The analysis showed how teacher strategies can create a context which is geared to the needs and abilities of some pupils at the expense of those of others. Assessments made in the classroom therefore objectified what were essentially outcomes of a differentiating process. The assessments contained within them measures of skills and attributes other than those being assessed.

C. *Assessment as a product of a wider field of social action.*
It allowed an examination of teacher perspectives and to relate elements of the teacher created contexts to factors beyond the classroom. This indicated that there are fundamental differences between teachers and their pedagogies which cannot be systematised in the pursuit of comparability of contexts.

What follows is an example of the application of the above analytic concepts of 'coping' and 'framing' to the context in which the attainment target of Writing was assessed in Year 1 of the cohort's primary education. It is a necessarily brief summary of a much fuller account (Filer, 1993a), but will serve to put some substantive flesh on the above description in A-C.

It is important to remember in the following that in the National Curriculum, Handwriting and Spelling are distinct attainment targets intended to be assessed separately from Writing.

Contexts of assessment of Writing

Teacher strategies

Bernstein (1971) points out that teacher expectations will be realised through the message system of pedagogy. In the Year 1 class under study, children's knowledge, perceptions and interests were not expected to feature to any great extent in the finished product of their writing. Rather, writing was used as a vehicle for what I have described above as 'curriculum knowledge'. These expectations were realised through the processes by which the teacher outlined the subject content in advance and reinforced it during the writing and marking processes. For example, it was the teacher's words rather than pupils' that went into the word bank on the blackboard as necessary to the task. In addition, pupil responses in first drafts that reflected the teacher expectations were corrected and clarified for making a fair copy. Pupil responses that fell outside of teacher expectations and that were unclear in meaning were not corrected or clarified but edited out of texts by the teacher in the marking of first drafts.

Analysing the context in terms of teacher coping strategies, Children were expected to write independently, largely relying on phonic knowledge for spellings. Independent writing meant that there were no opportunities for the production of text other than through children's technical skills of handwriting and spelling. For example, no support for drafting in the form of word processing or dictation was available. When not teaching the whole class the teacher adopted a fixed position at the end of a table of 'naughty' children for the surveillance of this group in particular. From this position she also heard readers and dealt with a queue with work to be marked.

Assessment as a product of teacher-created context

As stated in A above, an analysis of organisation and control strategies enabled me to be specific about ways in which pupil written responses and the assessments of their writing were products of the teacher-created context.

The most important criteria used by the Year 1 teacher in the assessment of pupil's writing was their ability to sequence their thoughts and hence sequence the content of their text. This as well as other criteria, clearly hinged on pupils' producing enough text on which to be assessed. Many in the class produced no more than a line or two consisting of a variation on a teacher-given sentence.

Failure to produce enough text on which to be assessed could be directly linked to classroom organisation. (There may, of course, have been other contributory causes.) Firstly, content was circumscribed by the teacher's control over knowledge in the discussion of the activity, the construction of the word bank and in the marking process. The task, therefore was not so much for pupils to sequence their own thoughts but rather that they should sequence those of the teacher. Failure to produce sufficient text could also be attributed to teacher strategies for the control of pupils which limited supportive contact with pupils. Other strategies such as the requirements for individual working and the reliance on phonic knowledge further limited what could be written.

A reading of the finished product of writing tasks showed the effects of the constraints. Texts were standardised with respect to content and there were no idiosyncratic responses with respect to style, tense or tone. This was evidenced across a range of curriculum subject matter, including that relating to children's personal experiences.

The analysis in terms of coping and framing thus allowed the relationship between context, responses and assessments to be made specific. Through such an analysis it can be seen that variations between classes and schools in the degree to which writing is used as a vehicle for curriculum knowledge, in the flexibility of teacher expectations with regard to the content of writing and in the degree to which it is used to express children's knowledge, perceptions and interests, could render as invalid any comparisons between schools on the basis of Writing assessment results. This difficulty is further compounded if, in addition to the possibility of limited knowledge contexts, one takes into account different levels of technical support for the writing task.

Assessment as a product of a differentiating process

The analysis that I have outlined above relates assessments to contexts. At the same time it also shows how those assessments contain within them measures of skills and attributes other than those being assessed. In the assessing of pupils writing it can be seen in the above that a hidden agenda was in operation whereby pupils' engagement with a given body of knowledge, as well as technical skill of spelling and handwriting, formed unacknowledged elements of the assessment process. In addition, assessment of their writing contained within them a measure of behavioural attributes.

In this latter respect, as with technical skills, the assessments were the outcome of a differentiating process whereby the teacher-created context was geared to the needs and abilities of some children at the expense of others. The context in which writing tasks were carried out was geared to those pupils, a group of about 12, whose spelling and handwriting skills meant that they could produce text independently of the teacher. The context was also geared to those most likely to be disruptive in the classroom. Strategies for the close control of this group of pupils meant that they had access to teacher support and were kept on-task by her. In contrast to both of these groups, another group of pupils, some 12 in number, spent a large portion of their time off-task. They were able to write little independently, had little access to teacher support and spent a lot of time chatting, arguing over equipment, rearranging hair styles, etc. Such minor deviancy came within the 'working consensus' (Pollard, 1985) of the classroom and, provided that it did not cause too much noise or disruption, though seen as regrettable, it was largely accepted by the teacher.

Assessments of writing, therefore, objectified as the achievements of pupils that which in reality was jointly achieved by pupil and teacher. They represented the outcome of a process whereby pupils were differentially supported by the teacher-organised features of the classroom context.

Assessment and the context beyond the classroom

As described above, an analysis in terms of 'coping strategies' establishes links between elements of the teacher-created context and biographical, social and institutional factors beyond the classroom. It illuminated the individual ways in which teachers respond to wider political and ideological initiatives and imperatives for change.

The background to the practice of this Year 1 teacher was located by her within a particular set of social class, ideological and professional identities relating to herself, her pupils and her colleagues. The practice was embedded in local knowledge of families and the community and the perception of her pupils as being somewhat socially and culturally deprived. It was also embedded in a view of herself as a good, traditional classroom teacher. Unlike those teachers seeking promotion who, it was felt, had to go along with new methods, she was not prepared to easily abandon her tried and tested methods.

Elements of her coping strategies which frequently conflicted with the introduction of new initiatives were those related to the control of pupils' behaviour. These coping strategies were of particular personal and professional significance for this teacher. She had a reputation with the headteacher, with colleagues and with parents for being 'good with the naughty ones'. The pedagogy deployed in this control pervaded every aspect of her practice, this being reflected, as with writing above, in the uniformity of a range of artefacts produced by the children. New assessment procedures which required a teacher's close attention to the process of pupils activities as well as to their product, could not easily be accommodated within existing classroom routines. They were perceived by the teacher as a threat to the good control which she maintained in the classroom and to the integrity of her practice. In addition they threatened her reputation and identity as a teacher.

An understanding of the origins of teachers' classroom strategies is fundamental to a study of the objectivity of teacher assessment. As it stands, the above description of a teacher's pedagogy can be read as a criticism of the teacher for limiting the contexts in which children are assessed. An analysis of classroom strategies from the teacher's point of view, and in terms of the problematic nature of change, showsthat there are fundamental differences between teachers that cannot be systematized out of existence in the pursuit of comparable contexts and objectivity in assessment processes.

In this paper I have shown the way in which I have developed three themes form the literature of the sociology of assessment. The development of these themes, through a holistic analysis of teachers' practices, shows that there are fundamental differences between teachers and their pedagogies which have an impact on pupil responses and hence on the assessments made of those responses. It re-affirms in the context of the National Curriculum and Teacher assessment what has consistently been said about classroom assessments: that they are inevitably context-related.

References

ABBOTT, D., BROADFOOT, P., CROLL, P., OSBORN, M., and POLLARD, A. (1994). 'Some sink, some float: National Curriculum Assessment and accountability', *British Educational Research Journal*, **29**, No 2.

ALEXANDER, R., ROSE, J., and WOODHEAD, C. (1992). *Curriculum Organisation and Classroom Practice in Primary Schools: a Discussion Paper*. London: Department of Education and Science.

ASSESSMENT OF PERFORMANCE UNIT (1986). 'Planning scientific investigation at age 11'. In HARLEN, W. (Ed.) *Science Report for Teachers, 8*. London: HMSO.

BECKER, H. S. (1952). 'Social class variations in the teacher-pupil relationship', *Journal of Educational Sociology*, **25**, 451-65.

BERNSTEIN, B. (1971). 'On the classification and framing of educational knowledge.' In: YOUNG, M.F.D. (Ed.) *Knowledge and Control*. West Drayton: Collier Macmillan.

BLACK, P. (1990). Lecture given to the Association for Science Education, Cardiff.

CHESHIRE, J. and JENKINS, N. (1990). 'Gender issues in the GCSE oral English examination: part I', *Language and Education*, **4**, 4, 261-92.

CHESHIRE, J. and JENKINS, N. (1991). 'Gender issues in the GCSE oral English examination: part II', *Language and Education*, **5**, 1, 19-40.

DEPARTMENT OF EDUCATION AND SCIENCE (1989a). *From Policy to Practice*. London: HMSO.

DEPARTMENT OF EDUCATION AND SCIENCE (1989b). *The Education Reform Act 1988: the School Curriculum and Assessment*. London: HMSO.

DEPARTMENT OF EDUCATION AND SCIENCE AND THE WELSH OFFICE (1990). *English in the National Curriculum*. London: HMSO.

DEPARTMENT OF EDUCATION AND SCIENCE (1991). *Assessment, recording and reporting*. Report by Her Majesty's Inspectorate for the first year 1989-90London: HMSO.

DOUGLAS, J.W.B. (1964). *The Home and the School*. London: MacGibbon & Kee.

EGGLESTON, J. (1988). 'The new Education Bill and Assessment: some implications for black children', *Multicultural Teaching*, **6**, 2, 24-5, 30.

FILER, A. (1993a). 'Contexts of assessment in a primary school classroom', *British Educational Research Journal.* **19**, 1, 95-107.

FILER, A. (1993b). 'The assessment of classroom language', *International Studies in Sociology of Education.* **3**, 2.

FILER, A. (1993c). Contexts of teacher assessment in a primary school. Unpublished PhD thesis.

FOUCAULT, M. (1971). 'Orders of discourse', *Social Science Information*, **10**, 2, 7-30.

FOUCAULT, M. (1980). 'Prison talk'. In: GORDON C. (Ed) *Power/Knowledge*. New York: Pantheon.

GOOD, T. L. and BROPHY, J. E. (1970). 'Teacher-child diadic interactions: a new method of classroom observation', *Journal of School Psychology*, **8**, 2, 131-138.

HARGREAVES, A. (1978). 'The significance of classroom coping strategies'. In: BARTON L. and MEIGHAN R. (Eds.) *Sociological Interpretations of Schooling and Classrooms: a Reappraisal.* Driffield: Nafferton.

HOFKINS, D. (1991). *The National Curriculum Update*, Summer, p4. London: Times Supplements Ltd.

HOFKINS, D. (1992). *The National Curriculum Update*, May, p10. London: Times Supplements Ltd.

JACKSON. B. (1964). *Streaming: An Education System in Miniature*. London: Routledge & Kegan Paul.

KEDDIE, N. (1971). 'Classroom knowledge'. In: YOUNG, M. F. D. (Ed.) *Knowledge and Control.* London: Collier Macmillan.

KRESS, G. (1985). ''Socio-linguistic development and the mature language user: different voices for different occasions'. In: WELLS, G. and NICHOLLS, J. (Eds) *Language and Learning*. Lewes, East Sussex: Falmer Press.

LEITER, K. C. W. (1974). 'Ad hocing in the schools'. In: CICOUREL, A.V. (Ed) *Language Use and School Performance.* New York: Academic Press.

LICHT, B.G., and DWECK, C.S., (1984). 'Determinants of academic achievement: the interaction of children's achievement orientation with skill area', *Developmental Psychology*, **20**, 4, 628-36.

MEHAN, H. (1973). 'Assessing children's school performance'. In: DREITZEL, H. P.(Ed.) *Childhood and Socialisation.* New York: Collier Macmillan.

MORTIMORE, P., SAMMONS, P., STOLL, L., LEWIS, D. and ECOB, R. (1988). *School Matters,* Wells: Open Books.

NASH, R. (1976). *Teacher Expectations and Pupil Learning.* London: Routledge & Kegan Paul.

POLLARD, A. (1985). *The Social World of The Primary School.* Eastbourne: Holt, Rinehart & Winston.

RIST, R. C. (1970). 'Student social class and teacher expectations: the self-fulfilling prophesy in ghetto education', *Harvard Educational Review.* **40**, 3, 411-511.

ROSENTHAL, R. and JACOBSEN, L. (1968). *Pygmalion in the Classroom.* New York: Holt Rinehart & Winston.

SCHOOL EXAMINATIONS AND ASSESSMENT COUNCIL (1989). *A Guide to Teacher Assessment.* London: HMSO.

SCHOOL EXAMINATIONS AND ASSESSMENT COUNCIL (1991). *Key Stage 1 Pilot 1990: a Report from the Evaluation and Monitoring Unit.* London, HMSO.

SHARP, R. and GREEN, A. (1975). *Education and Social Control.* London: Routledge & Kegan Paul.

SHORROCKS, D., DANIELS, S., FROBSHER, L., NELSON, N., WATERSON, A. and BELL, J. (1992). *Evaluation of National Curriculum Assessment at Key Stage 1.* London: School Examinations and Assessment Council.

SILBERMAN, M. L. (1969). 'Behavioral expressions of teachers' attitudes towards elementary school students', *Journal of Educational Psychology*, **60**, 5, 402-7.

VOLOSHINOV, V. N. (1973). *Marxism and the Philosophy of Language.* London; Seminar Press.

WALDEN, R. and WALKERDINE, V. (1985). *Girls and Mathematics from Primary to Secondary Schooling,* Bedford Way Papers, **24**. London: Institute of Education.

ZEICHNER, K. M., TABACHNICK, B. R. and DENSMORE, K. (1987). 'Individual, institutional and cultural influences on the development of teachers' craft knowledge.' In: CALDERHEAD, J. (Ed) *Exploring Teachers' Thinking.* London: Cassell Education Ltd.

CHAPTER 5

MEASURING AND EVALUATING RELIABILITY IN NATIONAL CURRICULUM ASSESSMENT

Alastair Pollitt, University of Cambridge

Abstract

The concept of test reliability has outlived its usefulness. Its traditional formulation is misleading, inappropriate and inadequate for modern assessment. It is unstable, not comparable across tests or tasks, and the ten-point scale (or any likely replacement for it) is too coarse to support the reliability statistic seen as a ratio of variances.

In *real* statistics, and *real* measurement, the emphasis is on quantifying error or the probability of error, and the reliability coefficient diverts attention from that proper concern in testing. There are many sources of variability in children's results, but reliability theory treats them all as error. A proper interpretation of a child's score – the public sense of 'reliable' – depends on seeing it in a richer context of knowledge about the child. The several purposes of National Curriculum Assessment correspond to different concerns for score variation, and the inability of reliability theory to address systematic sources of error means that reported results could suffer severely from bias.

Introduction

The traditional form of test theory, which developed gradually from beginnings around 1920 to its apotheosis in Lord and Novick (1968), has sometimes been named True Score Theory, and sometimes Reliability Theory, names which highlight the intimate relationship between indices of reliability and the concept of true score that underlies it. Although this conceptualisation of test scores has almost wholly disappeared from the technical literature on mental measurement, the concept of reliability which derived from it has not, and it continues to distort the interpretation of error in educational measurement. The system of national testing is a particularly inappropriate context for the concept of reliability, and so a particularly appropriate one for seeing its shortcomings.

Why assess reliability?

Every specialist discipline takes words from 'natural' language and gives them special meanings; examples include *power* or *energy* in physics, *power* or *integrate* in mathematics, *nominal* or *theme* in linguistics, *money* or *elastic* in economics. In each of these cases a naïve adult entering the specialism would need to unlearn the familiar meaning and then to learn the technical meaning, which is defined formally by an explicit definition. In other cases, such as *personality* in psychology, there is no agreed definition, and much argument even among specialists. So long as these words are used by competent specialists, aware of any differences between their respective definitions and in a spirit of cooperation, there may be no problem, but imagine the bizarre conversation if a physicist and a politician discussed *power* without recognising their different definitions. The specialist owes a duty to the public to make it clear when the words they use are not 'natural'.

Conversations about educational testing may be only a little less bizarre. Terminology is sometimes deliberately adopted with the intention of misleading the public and the politicians currently in power; the best example of this is surely *criterion.* Those who remember Keith Joseph as Secretary of State for Education will remember his enthusiasm for 'criterion-referenced testing'. Popham (1978, p 94) noted how popular the term was, and advocated continuing to use it while trying to 'influence those involved in this field to define the concept so that it is, indeed, equivalent with ... domain-referenced tests'.

Hambleton *et al.* endorsed this strategy in their 1978 review of criterion-reference research, writing (p 2) that it would be 'unfortunate' to stop using the word 'criterion'. Of course, the aim was to mislead politicians, and the general public, into believing that criterion-referenced testing in some way guaranteed that standards would be maintained: in fact, the effect has been almost exactly the opposite, as domain-referenced tests have singularly failed to address the issue of standards.

The main point is that every 'natural' word given a technical meaning brings with it a semantic baggage of connotations and associations. The specialist who imports a natural word should above all avoid arrogating too much. Of all the technical terms in educational measurement, the term *reliability* is the one most obviously guilty of arrogance; its technical definition as the ratio of true score variance to observed score variance captures very little of what most people assume is implied by it. I believe that, when our professional activity interacts with the 'real world', we must use natural meanings and meet reasonable natural assumptions. When we provide a public service, paid for by public funds, I believe these assumptions by the public become requirements that we are obliged to try to satisfy.

In natural language 'reliability', like 'criterion', is a word with connotations of quality. However, the process of technical definition has stripped the connotations from the word, leaving a definitional residue which only accidentally bears any resemblance to the natural meaning. This removes those very qualities that make it so attractive to those who oversee the education system.

Rather than try to define yet another technical term, let us, for the moment, return to the natural meaning; we can recognise two sorts of reason why it might be useful to evaluate the 'reliability' of National Curriculum (NC) assessments, one more summative and the other more formative, and these are discussed in the next two sections.

Evaluation of NC testing

In any official system that is supposed to be used publicly, there is an obvious concern about how well the system operates: Does it work well enough? It is of course a personal judgement how well is well enough, and the statistician must turn this into questions such as 'How likely is it that we have correctly assigned a Level to a child?' When we consider the range of assessments that are to be combined in the assigning of a Level to each child it is obvious that such a question can only be answered pragmatically, and *post hoc*. Traditional theory can provide an estimate of the standard error of a single assessment. It cannot, however, allow a proper estimation in advance, from characteristics of the various individual assessments, of the probability of error after aggregation of such a variety of components for, even if each component could be adequately evaluated, their distributions and interrelationships would be too complex to be adequately modelled under traditional assumptions of multivariate normality.

We are forced therefore to look to methods that quantify classification consistency rather than to traditional reliability. Levels actually awarded can be cross-tabulated with alternatives obtained by some other approach, such as reassessing the children or using the teachers' judgements, and the amount and nature of disagreement noted. We are then clearly entering the grey area between reliability and validity in the traditional conceptualisation, reintroducing some of the natural meaning of the word that traditional theory sought to remove.

It will be clear that 'reliability' in this sense can only apply at the end of NC Assessment, after aggregation is completed, as it is only then that classification takes place. This determines the level of detail at which the system can be evaluated; it must correspond to the level at which reporting takes place. If results are not reported at test or statement of attainment level, then it would be inappropriate to evaluate the system at any such small scale. On the other hand, if results are to be reported for each attainment target rather than for the whole subject, it will be inappropriate to evaluate the system at the scale of whole subjects.

Improvement of test quality

If the evaluation suggests that the system is not 'good enough' (and it is very likely to do so), concern will then shift to the smaller scale, or to the aggregation process. To improve the system, global indicators of quality must give way to local ones. It will be relatively easy to see whether any aspect of aggregation is causing a reduction in the replicability of the final Level, but more difficult to decide what to do about it. We may more easily (in principle at least) deal with problems caused by 'unreliable' components, where it is clear that we should seek ways to improve the quality of the assessment. The difficulty here is merely a serious practical one. It will, however, no doubt be argued that some component or other is essential to the curriculum even when it adds nothing to, or even subtracts from, the consistency of the overall assessment.

There are no simple rules for deciding when a component's 'reliability' is good enough. Some simple assessments will involve multiple judgements of a relatively objective kind, leading to results that will be more dependable, while others may only allow single subjective judgements. The dependability of the result will not normally reflect the perceived importance of each component, and aggregation will then not lead to assignments that 'validly' reflect the curricular intentions. Given the variety of test types and aggregation methods that may be used, the only way to evaluate a single assessment will be against a background of comparable 'reliability' measures. This is difficult when a test is new in format, but will become easy as more tests of the same kind are developed. It will always be very difficult to compare the 'reliabilities' of different components within an AT assessment if they are assessed in different ways.

Fortunately, as with Utopias, it is better not to try to design an ideal system, nor necessary to 'measure' the current one in order to see how to improve it. No one should hope to get a perfect system in place at the first attempt; we must be satisfied with a reasonable one and then aim to improve it piecemeal.

Standard error rather than reliability coefficient

Many of the problems with traditional conceptions of reliability are caused by the definition of the coefficient as a ratio of variances. Reliability is the central concept of traditional test theory, and a dangerously convenient 'measure' of a test's quality. The sensitivity of the coefficient to the range of ability in the sample of students is well known: add some idiots and a few geniuses and the alpha coefficient shoots up. One reading test widely used in British primary schools was able to claim a reliability coefficient of 0.975, 'good' by any standards, and 'better' than any of the old 11+ tests. How? By the simple trick of including three whole year groups of children in a single sample, and thereby grossly inflating the range of reading ability. More serious than such deceit in the NC context, however, is the effect of the scales being used. The traditional treatment of reliability requires a long, ideally a continuous rather than a discrete, numerical scale of equal intervals, although it works reasonably well with traditional test score scales so long as the students' scores are distributed reasonably normally. But in NC Assessment we will frequently find that the distribution of Level assignments is almost dichotomous, with more than 80 per cent of students falling into a pair of adjacent bands, and traditional reliability coefficients were not designed for this.

It is worth noting at this point that reliability theory is not a central concept of statistical theory, and that many professional statisticians have never heard of 'reliability' in this sense. In retrospect, reliability theory will come to be seen as a temporary aberration with which a subgroup of applied psychologists and educators deluded themselves that they were estimating the accuracy of measurement instruments. The proper choice should have been to concentrate on estimating inaccuracy.

What else are these coefficients used for? When they are not being compared, supposedly to 'judge' the quality of different tests, reliability coefficients are used only to estimate what is called the standard error of measurement, or SEM. A more mainstream statistical treatment estimates error directly, and there are several techniques for doing so. In the last period of traditional theory, especially under Frederick Lord at ETS, it was realised that the assumption that one SEM could apply at every score was obviously untenable, and considerable effort was put into developing regression techniques for estimating the error associated with measurements at different points along the test score scale. More recently, explicit latent trait models of test performance have been developed which provide direct ways of calculating an estimation error for each score, (Birnbaum, in Lord and Novick (1968); Rasch,1960; Wright and Stone, 1979), but it is unlikely that these can yet be applied to the fruit salad of assessments that will jointly define a NC assignment of Levels. Decision classification tables provide another, more 'top down', approach. It is important to note that the NC reporting scale was predefined by TGAT to be equal interval with respect to time, with each level corresponding to two years of the average child's life. However this may be revised, two consequences are almost certain: the reporting scale will almost certainly not be equal interval with respect to developing ability, and the measurement error will be different at different boundaries between Levels.

This suggests two conclusions. First, for evaluating the system, counts of decision concordance and estimates of the probabilities of correct assignment to Levels should be used as a way of estimating how much confidence we can have in each reported result. Second, in test design it will often be possible to utilise estimates of measurement error at important criterion scores, using some kind of latent trait model.

Person variance: how a child's Level varies with time

So far we have considered problems of judging assessment error within the traditional conception of reliability, and with some alternative conceptions of error. We have still, however, accepted one aspect of the traditional approach, by considering everything within the context of a single test. There is more to it than that.

The context of NC Assessment will be that schools carry out assessment of children at the end of each key stage, and perhaps more frequently. Reliability, as usually conceived, would compare measurement error to the variance of observed scores across a group of children on each attainment target, but it could equally logically be defined as a comparison of measurement error to the variance of scores across key stages within children. That is, it can be looked at as an indicator of how accurately the system charts development: public confidence in the 'reliability' of the assessments will be undermined if children do not usually show the expected pattern of improvement across key Stages.

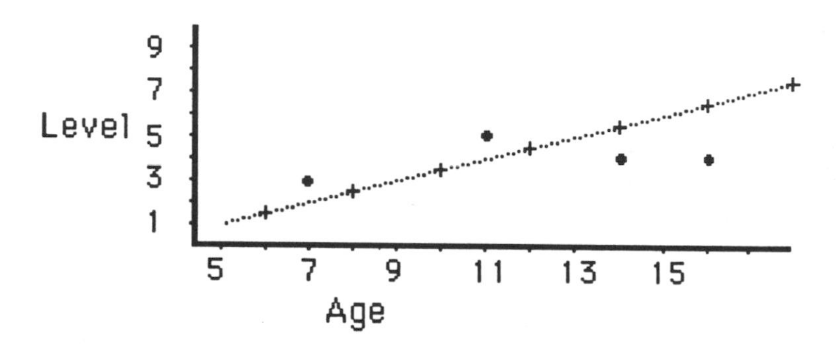

This argument will apply whatever scale results are reported on and whatever pattern of testing or assessment is eventually adopted. It will be important to monitor results to see the typical patterns that show up and the frequency of 'bizarre' patterns. Medical researchers and doctors are able to use well-established patterns of expected growth for a variety of features of the human body, but psychological research has been more disappointing; even in the most researched areas of cognition the accuracy of measurement is so low that plots of individual 'growth' cannot be produced with sufficient clarity to be useful, or to enable us to identify aberrant patterns. The continuing controversies about sex differences in cognitive development, when contrasted with the consensus over sex differences in patterns of physical growth, illustrate the problem. Nevertheless, once the system begins to stabilise, the pattern of an individual child's AT assessments over time will be seen as an important indicator of any unreliability in NC Assessment.

What is the main purpose of NC assessment?

Despite repeated advice to the contrary, government still seems to believe that one system of national tests can fulfil many functions. Charting cognitive development, diagnosing individual problems, reporting to parents, scrutinising schools and monitoring national standards are all declared to be important roles for the tests to play. It is a fundamental principle of test design that each testing purpose needs a different sort of test and a different sort of testing system if sufficient accuracy is to be achieved. By way of analogy, it is fortunate that aeronautical, marine and automobile engineers do not design their vehicles in this global way, and strange that government cannot see the folly that they are creating - 'Concorde: the Hovercraft'? The rest of this paper considers three aspects of measurement error that are substantially different when national testing is considered as serving different purposes.

Reliable person scores or 'reliable' school means?

It is traditional to consider that reliability concerns a single student's score, and the degree of unreliability is indicated by the standard error of that score. The previous section noted that NC Assessment is likely to be quite unreliable in this respect – certainly more unreliable than O-levels were, and GCSEs are, since the testing conditions will be less standardised, and markers will be less trained. When we look at the *differences* between two such unreliable NC assessments made by different teachers two or three years apart, and remember that a child is only expected to progress by one Level in every two years, it is obvious that the differences will be very unreliable: the potential for 'BIZARRE NC RESULTS' (to paraphrase a famous *Times Educational Supplement* headline) is enormous.

If, however, the focus is on school results, as seems to be implied by the political emphasis on school league tables, and if it is assumed (as is usual) that this unreliability is due to random error, then the problem becomes far less serious. Since the school mean will usually be based on at least 25 cases in primary schools and far more in secondary schools, random measurement error in the mean will probably be small.

In this respect, accurate comparison of schools' results in league tables will be feasible. There are two other serious problems, though, which are not so easily overcome.

Comparability

Textbooks often recommend 'parallel forms' or 'equivalent forms' measures of reliability for educational contexts. These are simply the correlation between two supposedly parallel or equivalent tests; it is a well known characteristic of correlation coefficients that they are quite oblivious to differences in the standard, that is the difficulty, of the two tests. But it does often matter, does it not, whether one test is easier than the other which is supposed to be 'equivalent' to it? Test agencies know this as the problem of 'horizontal equating'. School examination boards have developed elaborate procedures for trying to ensure that the papers they set each year are just as difficult as those in earlier years, and that the standard of severity amongst markers is maintained constant, yet they still find it necessary to carry out some *post hoc* adjustment in the light of observed results. This will be very difficult in NC Assessment. If the NC tests are to be of any use in monitoring national standards of achievement – and the public expect that they will be – it will be vital to ensure accurate equating of difficulty from year to year.

A similar issue arises in monitoring individuals' development, in addition to the unreliability problem discussed in the previous section. As children pass from one key stage to the next it would seem essential that their attainment keeps its value, that is, that a Level 5 in KS3 should mean the same standard as Level 5 at KS2. So far there has been no attempt to ensure this 'vertical equating' of national tests.

The problems of comparability between different subjects present even more dangers. Already this year we have seen the serious national press printing such absurd headlines as 'PUPILS DO BETTER AT MATHS THAN SCIENCE', and the public clearly expect that a '6' in maths will 'mean' the same as a '6' in science, or English or anything else. This expectation must either be squashed from the outset or planned for. Since English employers have always treated all subjects equally, as in the traditional 'five O-levels' demand, squashing the expectation now seems doomed, and we ought therefore to try to find some way of equating standards across subjects.

There is one way by which this could be done which was not easily available for older examinations. Since these tests relate to a National Curriculum, (almost) every child will be tested on every test, and it would be possible to equate them empirically by ensuring that the same proportion of children are at each level in each subject. (At least this would be easy so long as a child is given a total test score by adding up their separate question scores.) This sort of horizontal equating procedure underlies many well-known tests giving standardised profiles (e.g. Edinburgh Reading Tests, British Ability Scales). We have in national testing a classic case of a criterion-referenced system that needs normative information in order to set its criteria in a way that will not mislead the public.

Unless this sort of equating is carried out, it will not be reasonable to expect an average child to show a 'flat profile' across subjects. Consider the consequences, by asking how a parent should interpret the following profile:

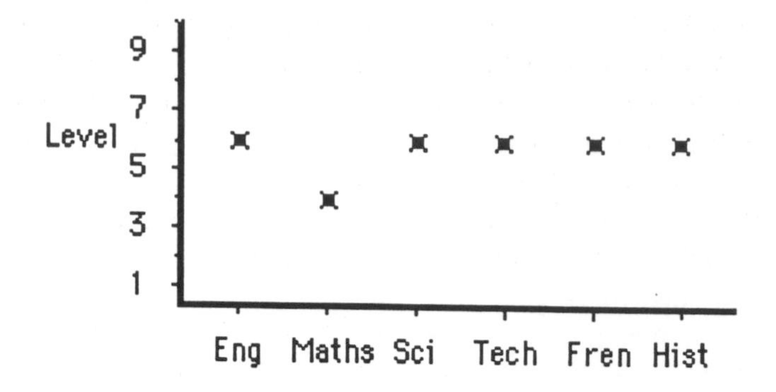

Is it fair to conclude that this child is *poorer* at maths than at other subjects? Not unless all of the test in these subjects have been equated horizontally; otherwise it could simply be that the maths test was harder than the others.

In general, comparability of standards - within one AT or subject from year to year, between subjects, and across Key Stages - will turn out to be a much more serious problem than test unreliability as traditionally conceived.

Profit, loss and bias in measurement error

Poor equating means that all results on one particular test are systematically raised or suppressed compared to those from another, supposedly equivalent, test. There is another source of systematic error that must be a cause for even more concern than this.

Whatever the effect on their self-esteem, there is little serious loss to an individual child if they are over- or under-assessed by one Level. Teachers will quickly learn that some '5's are better than some '6's, despite their doing less well in the formal assessment. In a climate of accountability and competition there will, however, be considerable profit to a school at KS2 if all of its children are over-assessed by the same amount, and even more if the school simultaneously under-assesses all of the children at KS1, for in these circumstances the 'value added' in the intervening years will be maximised. Try to imagine the discussions that might take place in primary school staffrooms as upper school teachers try to persuade their lower school colleagues to underestimate children's levels so as to make the school as a whole look good.

Errors of this sort are systematic, not random, and to a statistician they are examples of what is called *bias* in the measurement system. There is not any derogatory intention in saying that teachers' assessments will be biased, for while deliberate bias of the sort suggested above is possible, unintended bias is inevitable in such an unstandardised system. Training teachers in NC assessment will reduce these biases somewhat by helping them understand the consensus meaning of the criteria, but many sources of bias will remain. Whenever individual administration and subjective judgements are used, the testing conditions will not be the same in every school, and some of these differences will be systematically in favour of or against those children. The main concern of the auditors whose duty is to moderate assessments should be to look for systematic rather than random errors in the assessments.

Once again, traditional estimates of reliability fail, for they cannot detect systematic deviations between two sets of measures. Auditors will need to develop a systematic way to spot systematic error. There is a world of a difference between one teacher whose estimates are one Level high half of the time and one Level low the other half and another teacher whose estimates are always one Level high. The first teacher is 'unreliable' in traditional terms while the latter is 'reliable'; paradoxically the former will provide an accurate school mean while the latter will inflate it by one whole Level. The effects of bias in NC testing will be insidious.

Unlike random error, statistical bias is not reduced by sample size, since its source is common to every person in a particular sample. Thus one teacher who consistently overestimates or underestimates students' Levels, even by a small amount, will significantly change the school's placing in any league table. Systematic 'error' attributable to teachers or schools or auditors will almost certainly swamp individual measurement error when we consider school means.

Conclusion

To sum up, the chief threat to the credibility of NC league tables is not variation in social mix, or the inadequacy of the tests or markers, nor lack of reliability in the instruments, but the inevitable and probably undetectable sources of systematic statistical bias introduced into the assessment process by the lack of standardisation of teachers and auditors.

The chief threat to the reliability of the NC Assessment system, in the natural sense of the word, is the failure to ensure that the many tests that report on the same scale are in any sense equivalent.

We are in danger of implementing a system of tests that behave like thermometers, all pretending to measure on the Celsius scale, but which actually each have their own freezing point and each their own idea of what constitutes a nice summer's day.

References

HAMBLETON, R. K., SWAMINATHAN, H., ALGINA, J. and COULSON, D. B. (1978). 'Criterion-referenced testing and measurement: a review of technical issues and developments', *Review of Educational Research*, **48**, 1-47.

LORD, F. M. and NOVICK, M. R. (1968). *Statistical Theories of Mental Test Scores*. Reading, Mass: Addison-Wesley.

POPHAM, W. J. (1978). *Criterion-Referenced Measurement*. Englewood Cliffs, NJ: Prentice-Hall.

RASCH, G. (1960). *Probabilistic Models for Some Intelligence and Attainment Tests*. Copenhagen: Danmarks Paedagogiske Institut. (Reprinted 1980, Chicago: University of Chicago Press.)

WRIGHT, B. D. and STONE M. H. (1979). *Best Test Design*. Chicago: MESA Press.

CHAPTER 6

GRAPHICAL REPRESENTATION OF THE RELIABILITY OF NATIONAL CURRICULUM ASSESSMENT

Ian Schagen
National Foundation for Educational Research

Synopsis

The reliability or reproducibility of NCA is not usefully represented by a single statistic, depending as it does on a complex interaction between the SoAs, the aggregation method and the aptitude of the individual pupil. Graphical representations, based on probabilistic models of pupil attainment and item difficulties, allow the performance of the NCA test to be seen as a function of pupil potential attainment. Examples of such graphs will be given, with discussion of the forms expected for 'ideal' NCA tests. The models used in developing these graphs have been validated through the use of simulated data.

Introduction

The term 'reliability' is used as a desirable measure for NCA, by analogy with the usage in conventional, norm-referenced psychometric tests, for which it is reasonably well-defined. The situation for NCA is not the same, as has been argued in several places (see e.g. Hutchison and Schagen, 1991; Schagen, 1993). An alternative and perhaps looser term for what we are trying to measure is 'reproducibility' - the extent to which the NCA overall outcome could be reproduced under different circumstances. For the sake of argument, we shall continue to use the term 'reliability', with the understanding that it is not defined precisely for NCA. The other important concept — 'validity' — the extent to which the outcome assigned by NCA is the 'right' one for the pupil — we shall not attempt to discuss in this paper.

In conventional testing a single statistic, the reliability coefficient, is frequently regarded as being sufficient information on this subject. Even here this may not be so; it is conceivable that a test may be more reliable at one end of the ability range than the other. For NCA the situation is such that it is unlikely that any single statistic could sensibly encapsulate the complex interactions between the items, the aggregation rule and the performance of the individual pupil. This is particularly the case because the objective of NCA is to assign each pupil to a certain discrete Level in the attainment target of interest. Thus certain pupils may be assigned quite clearly to a single Level, while others who are 'borderline' will inevitably be more unreliably assigned.

The thrust of this argument is that to evaluate the reliability of a particular NCA test, the measures used will be graphical or functional rather than purely numerical.

Modelling pupil outcomes

The basic situation to be modelled relates to the assessment of a single attainment target (AT) by means of a test or standard task comprising a number of items. An aggregation rule defines how the outcomes of these items are combined to give an AT Level for each pupil. The essential requirement of a model is that it should be as simple as possible, but should fit this real situation. It should include the following features:

1. Item difficulties, to allow for items at the same nominal Level having different probabilities of being passed.
2. Pupil potential attainment values, so that pupils have different probabilities of passing items.
3. A link function, including uncertainty, which defines the probability of a pupil with given potential attainment passing an item of given difficulty.
4. The aggregation rule, as defined, to derive AT Levels from item results.

Models with the first three features are commonly used in the analysis of educational and psychometric tests — some of the most popular are grouped together under the title 'Item Response Theory' (IRT — see Lord and Novick, 1968, pp 399ff). These models use a logistic link function to derive the probability of an individual passing an item, and the uncertainty in the model is derived from parameters associated with the items.

In NCA, on the other hand, there seems to be some evidence that the uncertainty in the model would be better associated with individuals rather than items. Some individuals seem to perform predictably, passing items at or below a given Level and failing those above. Others are very erratic, failing Level 1 items and passing with ease those at Level 3. For these reasons, and because there seemed to be no valid reason for preferring the logistic function to the Normal integral function, a simple Normal model was developed whose link function is given by:

$$p_{ij} = \Phi((\mu_j - d_i) / \sigma_j) \qquad (1)$$

where p_{ij} = Probability that pupil j passes item i

μ_j = Mean potential attainment of pupil j

d_i = Difficulty of item i

σ_j = Attainment s.d. for pupil j.

Further details of this model and how it is fitted to NCA data are given in Schagen (1993). One of the issues to be resolved is the extent to which the details of the model influence the results obtained by using it. In other words, would a vastly different outcome be obtained from the use of an IRT-type model rather than the Normal model described above? This question is explored later in the paper.

Assigned Level variance functions

The best graphical representation of the reliability or reproducibility of NCA is a plot of the variance in the assigned Level as a function of pupil potential attainment. This plot gives an immediate picture of the behaviour of the test over the range of pupil abilities, and can be computed for a variety of currently-used aggregation rules.

In order to interpret such a plot, it is first useful to consider the form expected from an 'ideal' NCA test. As pupil potential attainment increases from a low value, we would expect the pupil's assigned Level to change from 'W' to Level 1. At the point where there is a 50 per cent chance of being assigned Level 1, the variance in the assigned Level will be 0.25. We should thus expect a series of sharp 'spikes', each rising to 0.25, at all the change-over points from one Level to the next. The width of the spikes can be regarded as a measure of how sharply the test distinguishes each Level from the next. Figure 1 shows the plot for AT Ma3 from the KS1 pilot data in 1990, which gives a picture which is not totally different from the ideal plot.

It is not clear a priori where exactly on the potential attainment scale we should expect the spikes to be located. The attainment scale is set up on the basis of the probabilities of passing individual items — for example, a value of 2.0 implies that the pupil has a 50 per cent chance of passing a correctly positioned Level 2 item. This means that we should probably want the transition from being awarded Level 1 to being awarded Level 2 to be at a point on the scale rather higher than 2.0, but below 3.0. This exposes a whole area of uncertainty — the relationship between performance based on individual items, and the award of Levels using aggregation rules. One of the uses of the variance plots is to illustrate this relationship.

As an example of these variance plots, consider the attainment target Ma 3 ('Number') under the old Mathematics structure, as it was assessed at KS1 from 1990 to 1992. The 1990 assessment was a pilot exercise, with three different sets of materials, and the variance curves derived from each of these are shown in Figures 1 to 3. In 1991 and 1992 a single task was used, and Figures 4 and 5 show the results in these years. As mentioned above, Figure 1 is the closest to the ideal curve. On the other hand, Figure 2 shows almost no distinction between Levels 2 and 3. Figure 3 is more reasonable, but shows some tendency for Levels 1 and 2 to be blurred. In both 1991 and 1992 (Figures 4 and 5) there is evidence of the merging of the 1/2 boundary and the 2/3 boundary, as in Figure 2. Note that in 1992, for the first time, Level 4 was available at KS1.

These variance functions therefore seem to be valuable tools for describing the behaviour of NCA tests, in particular the discrimination at the boundary between one Level and the next. However, the derivation of the function is heavily dependent on fitting a particular form of model to the data, and there remains the question of the the extent to which the function is an artefact of the model fitted. Another issue concerns the effect of 'adaptive' testing, as adopted for KS1 in 1992 and 1993, on the process.

Use of simulation studies to validate model fitting and variance functions

In the 1990 pilot tasks for KS1, each pupil was intended to attempt every item. Many did not, but missing items were normally grouped by activities rather than Levels and it was not completely unreasonable to treat them as randomly distributed. The 1991 and 1992 tasks allowed pupils to attempt only subsets of the items, depending on their 'entry point' (based on the teacher assessment) and final Level. Items at Levels which are not relevant to the pupil's performance are not attempted. It is not valid to assume that missing values are sparse and randomly distributed through the data.

The use of 'paths' through the assessment will affect parameter estimation when fitting the model. Since 'off-path' items are not attempted, there is a lower chance of very anomalous behaviour being detected, and this will lead to lower estimates of parameters associated with pupil performance variation. To investigate this and other issues a set of simulation exercises was carried out.

Each such exercise involved randomly generating item difficulties, with values spread about their nominal Levels. Pupils were also simulated, with their potential attainment values randomly distributed across the Levels. For each pupil, the outcome of each item could be computed according to the model in force, taking into account the item difficulty, pupil potential attainment and the element of uncertainty. In addition to this full set of item outcomes, it was possible to create a set of 'on-path' results, with items which would not have been encountered by the pupil set to missing. To determine such items, the 'entry point' was taken as the integer part of the potential attainment and the KS1 rules were followed to determine the path through the assessment and the final assigned Level.

To get a simulated analogue to the variance function, pupils are assigned to small 'bands' of potential attainment (each of width 0.1 Levels) and within each band it is a simple matter to compute the variance of the assigned Level. We can thus plot an 'empirical' assigned Level variance function which should be directly comparable with the curves obtained from the model-fitting exercise. Both sets of item data — the full item data and the 'on path' data — can be fed into the model-fitting software and estimated variance functions derived.

A number of simulation exercises were run, using the above strategy to compute both 'empirical' and estimated variance curves. Several different AT structures were assumed for this exercise, as well as two different aggregation rules. These rules are labelled 'KS1' and 'KS3', as they relate to the rules in force in 1992 for the testing of Key Stages 1 and 3.

KS1: To pass a Level with n SoAs tested at that Level, n-1 of the SoAs must be passed. The highest Level passed is awarded.

KS3: Every SoA at a Level must be passed to gain the Level, but if half or more of the SoAs at a Level are passed and sufficient SoAs at higher Levels have been passed, it is possible to be awarded the Level via 'rollback'.

Structure	No. of items	No. of levels	No of Items at each level	Aggregation method
A	9	3	3 - 3 - 3	KS1
B	12	4	2 - 4 - 2 - 4	KS1
C	8	4	2 - 2 - 2 - 2	KS3
D	12	4	3 - 3 - 3 - 3	KS1

In addition, it was decided to take the opportunity to carry out some sensitivity analysis on the exact form of the model used to generate the data. The default option is clearly to use exactly the same model to generate the data as is used in the software to fit and estimate the variance curve. This leaves the method open to criticism that nothing has been proved about the robustness of the model under variant forms of data. Four different models were therefore used to generate the simulated data.

1. **(N)** Normal model, as used in model fitting. The probability of a pupil passing an item is given by equation (1) above.

2. **(U)** Uniform model, with uncertainty associated with pupils, as in the above model. The probability of pupil j passing item i is given by:

$$p_{ij} = (\mu_j + \sigma_j - d_i) / (2\sigma_j) \qquad (2)$$

or 0 if < 0

or 1 if > 1

3. **(LI)** Logistic model, with uncertainty associated with items. This is equivalent to the IRT model. The probability of pupil j passing item i is given by:

$$p_{ij} = \exp\{a_i(\mu_j - d_i)\} / (1 + \exp\{a_i(\mu_j - d_i)\}) \quad (3)$$

4. **(LP)** Logistic model, with uncertainty associated with pupils. The probability of pupil j passing item i is given by:

$$p_{ij} = \exp\{a_j(\mu_j - d_i)\} / (1 + \exp\{a_j(\mu_j - d_i)\}) \quad (4)$$

A number of simulation exercises have been carried out, using different combinations of AT structures and models for data generation, with 2000 cases generated each time. For the KS1 AT structures (A, B and D) the modelled variance function was estimated using both the full item data and the item data truncated taking into account 'paths' through the SAT. For the KS3 structure (C) full item data only was assumed. Figures 6 to 9 show some example plots, comparing the 'empirical' variance function with those generated by the model. These examples have not been chosen to show the 'best fit', but to demonstrate the full range of matches obtained with a variety of structures and models.

Results of simulations

Studying these and other simulation runs, we may make the following observations:

1. There is little consistent difference between the four different models used to generate the simulated data in terms of the goodness of fit of the 'base model'. This implies that the exact structure of the underlying model is not an important feature — what counts is that it should contain parameters reflecting pupil ability, item difficulty, and uncertainty of outcomes.

2. Generally, the empirical variance functions from the simulations tend to reach higher peaks than those derived from the model. The overall functional shapes, however, are in general very close.

3. The locations of peaks in the functions on the potential attainment scale are not always in agreement. The reason for this is that when the base model is fitted, there is a constraint that the average item difficulty is equal to the average nominal level. No such constraint exists when item difficulties are randomly generated for the simulated data, which explains the discrepancies which are observed.

4. Overall, the variance curve fitted to the data seems to give an acceptable representation of the true situation. This is even the case when only partial item data is presented, and tends to validate this approach for 'adaptive' tests.

Other graphical representations

This paper has so far dealt exclusively with the variance function as a means of displaying the reliability or otherwise of NCA. There are, however, other related functions which may be plotted to give insights into the behaviour of these assessments. As well as the variance in the assigned Level, we may plot the mean assigned Level as a function of pupil potential attainment. Ideally, we should expect a 'step function' result for this, as the assessment is basically a system for transforming a continuous range of ability or potential attainment into a discrete set of Levels. If this is carried out effectively, at the 'transition point' from one Level to the next, we should expect a sudden jump, followed by a section in which the mean assigned Level is constant. In practice, however, this tends not to occur.

Figure 10 shows the mean assigned Level functions for the three different tasks of the 1990 KS1 Pilot. None of them shows a clear step-like function, although 'Myself' comes closest (compare Figure 1). 'Toys and Games' has a step at Level 1, but none at Level 2 (compare Figure 2). 'World About Me' shows a trace of a step at Level 2, but even less at Level 1 (compare Figure 3).

An alternative way of representing the performance of the assessment is in terms of the probabilities of passing each Level as functions of the underlying potential attainment. An example of such a plot is shown as Figure 11, for Ma 3 in the 1990 Pilot task 'Toys and Games'. Here we can see the overlap between the regions for passing Levels 2 and 3, which leads to the lack of a clear boundary between them, as illustrated in Figure 2. In general, however, the variance plots are simpler to interpret in terms of the reliability or reproducibility of the assessment.

Acknowledgements

This work is part of an ESRC-sponsored research project 'Reliability and related characteristics of adaptive testing in the context of National Curriculum Assessment' (Research grant: R 000 234137).

The author wishes to acknowledge the cooperation of the School Examinations and Assessment Council in giving permission to use data collected as part of the evaluation of National Curriculum Assessment. He also wishes to thank his colleagues for their help and advice, in particular Dougal Hutchison, Chris Whetton, Graham Ruddock and Marian Sainsbury.

References

HUTCHISON, D. and SCHAGEN, I. (1991). 'Reliability and allied measurements for criterion referened assessment', Final report to the ESRC.

LORD, F.M. and NOVICK, M.R. (1968) *Statistical Theories of Mental Test Scores*, Reading, Mass:, Addison-Wesley.

SCHAGEN, I.P. (1993) 'Problems in measuring the reliability of National Curriculum Assessment in England and Wales', *Educational Studies*, **19**, 1.

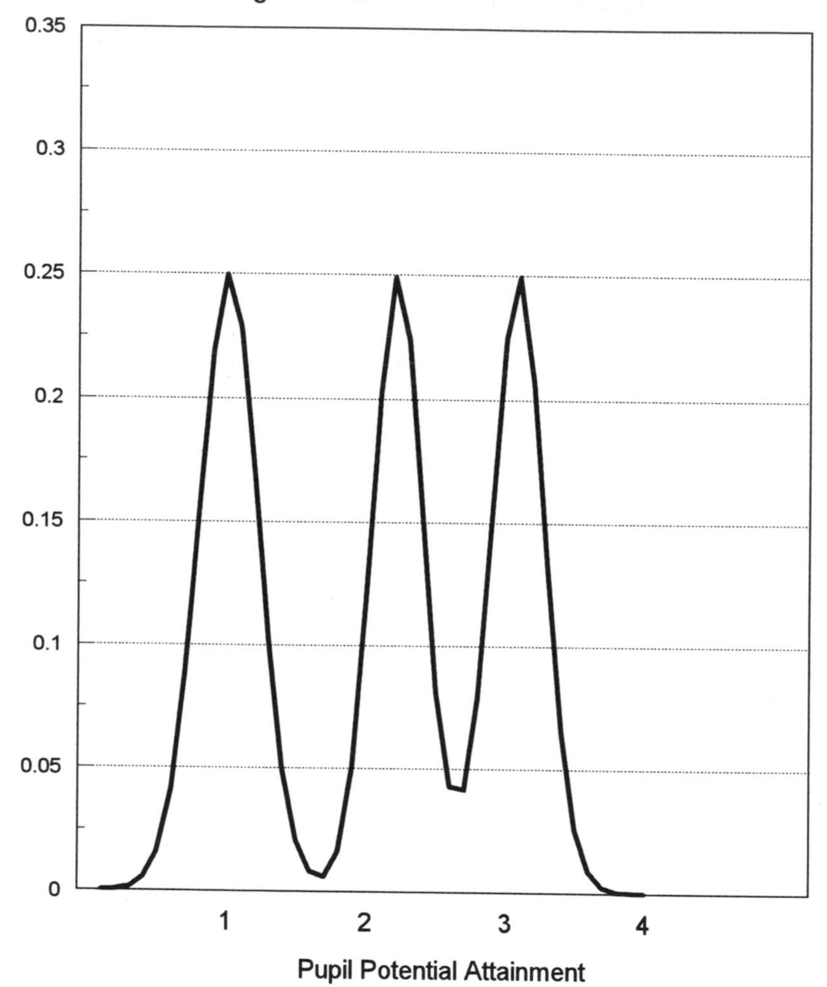
Figure 1
KS1 SAT Pilot 1990 - 'Myself'
Attainment Target Ma 3
Variance of assigned level
0.35
0.3
0.25
0.2
0.15
0.1
0.05
0
1
2
3
4
Pupil Potential Attainment

Figure 2

KS1 SAT Pilot 1990 - 'Toys & Games'

Attainment Target Ma 3

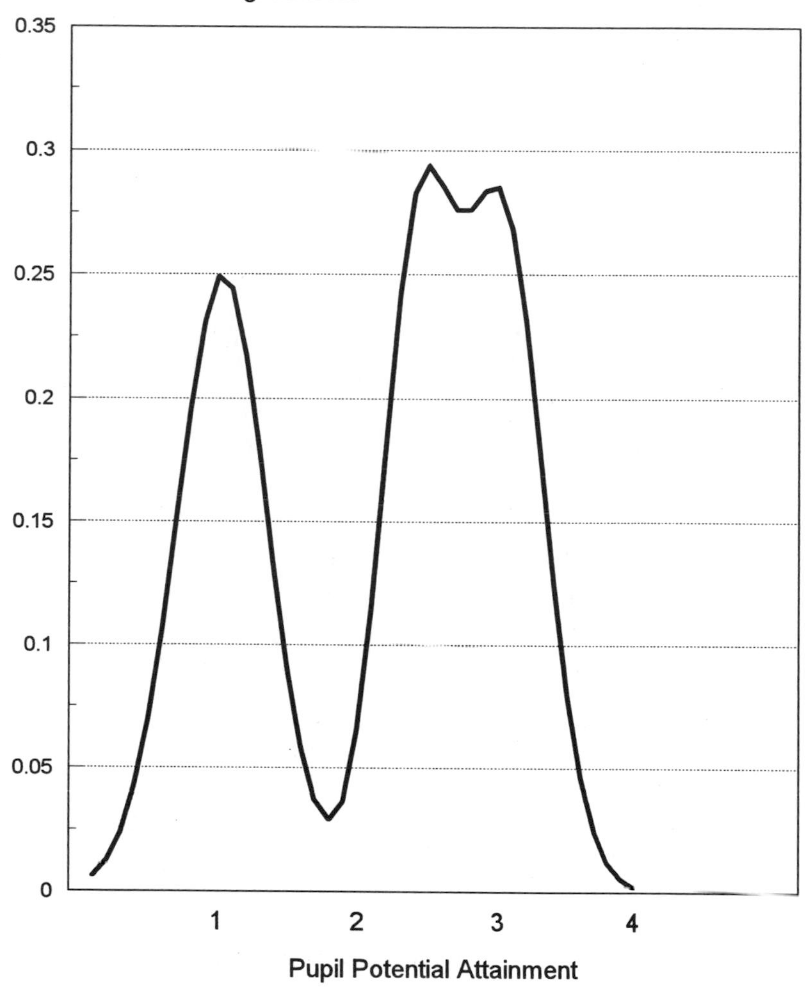

Figure 3

KS1 SAT Pilot 1990 - 'World About Me'

Attainment Target Ma 3

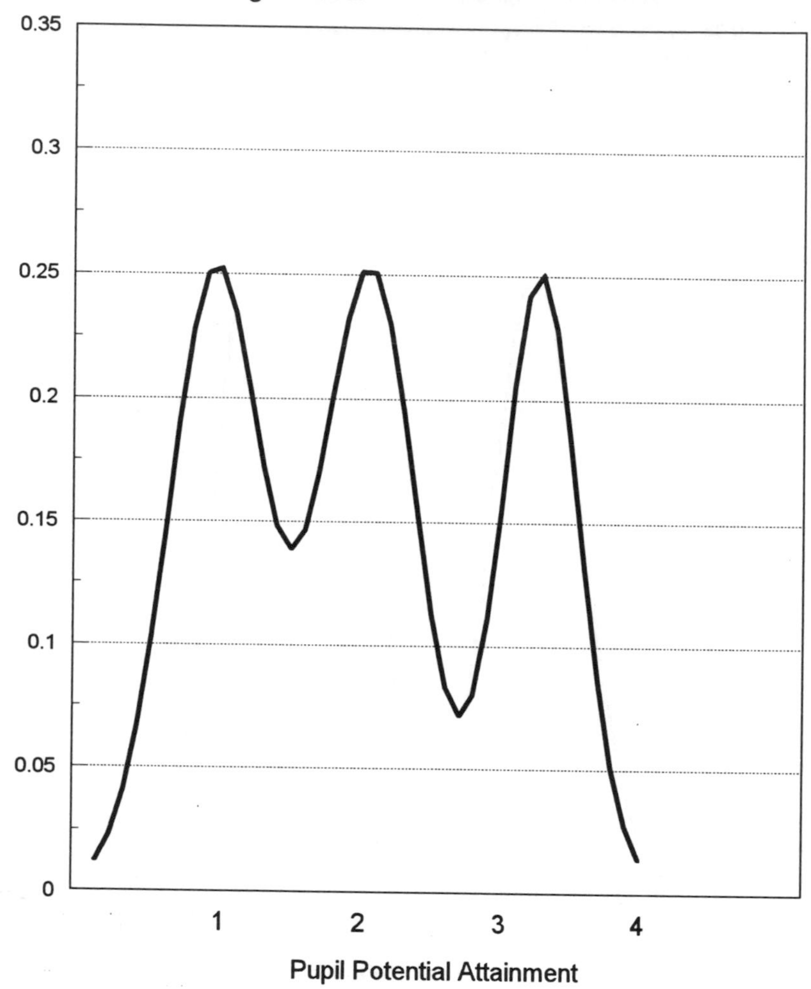

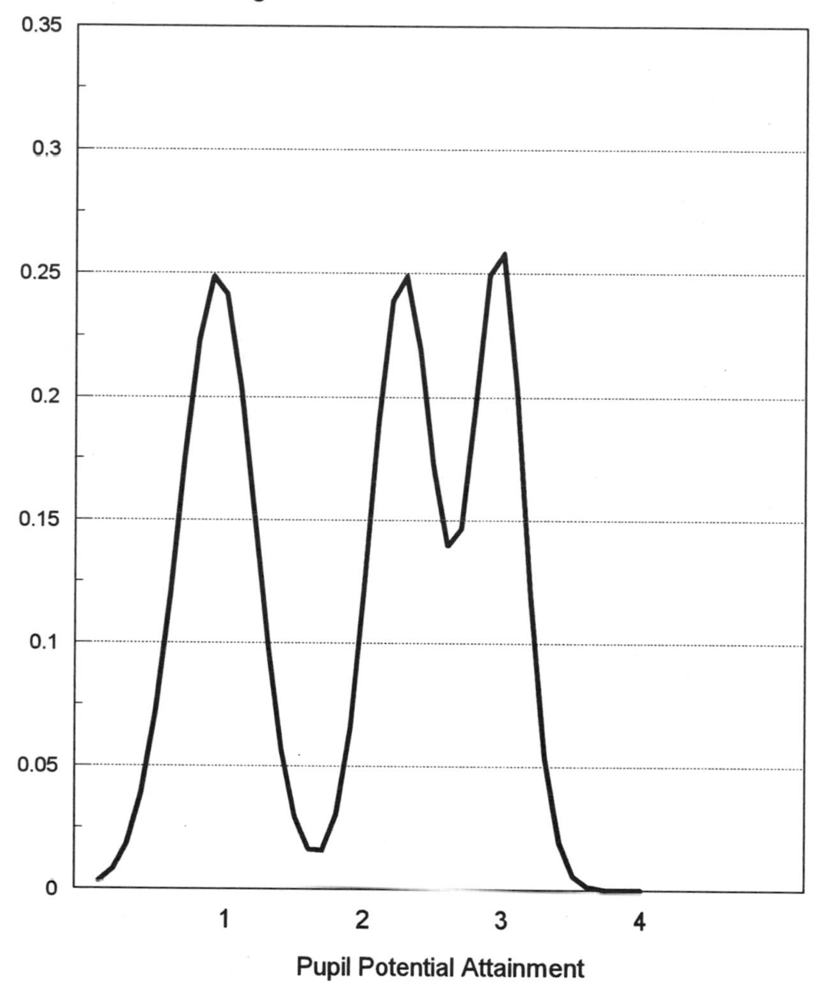
Figure 4
KS1 SAT Evaluation 1991
Attainment Target Ma 3
Variance of assigned level
0.35
0.3
0.25
0.2
0.15
0.1
0.05
0
1
2
3
4
Pupil Potential Attainment

Figure 5

KS1 SAT Evaluation 1992

Attainment Target Ma 3

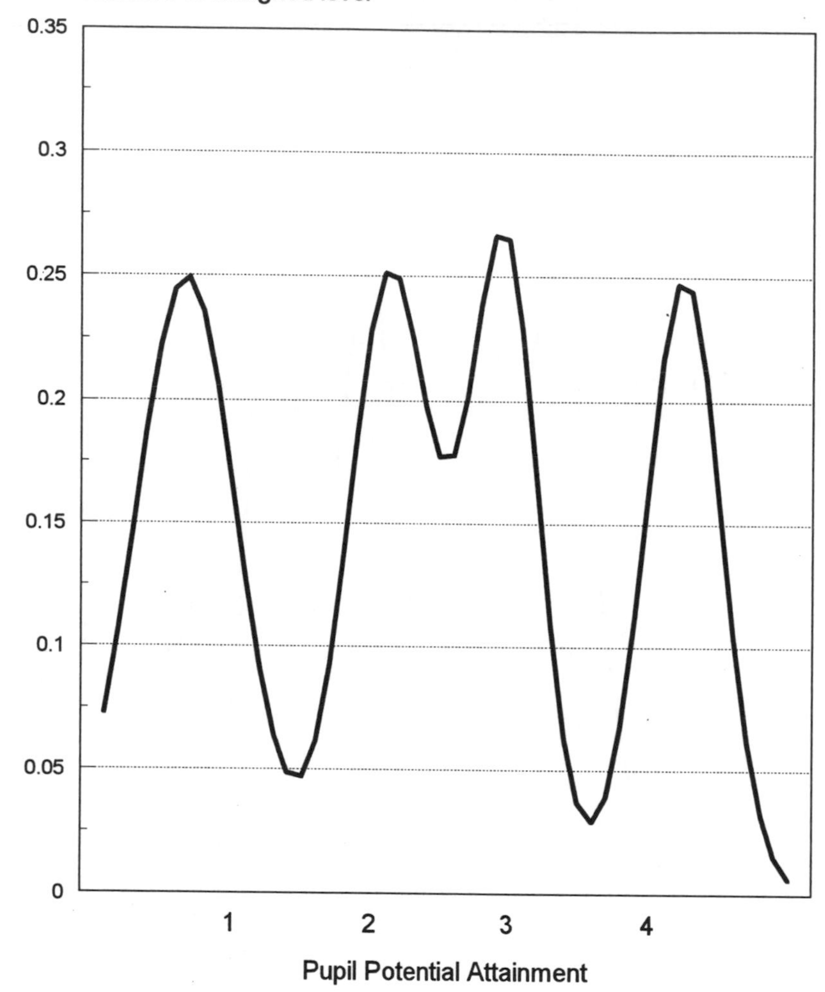

Figure 6

Attainment Target Structure A

Simulated data generated from Model N

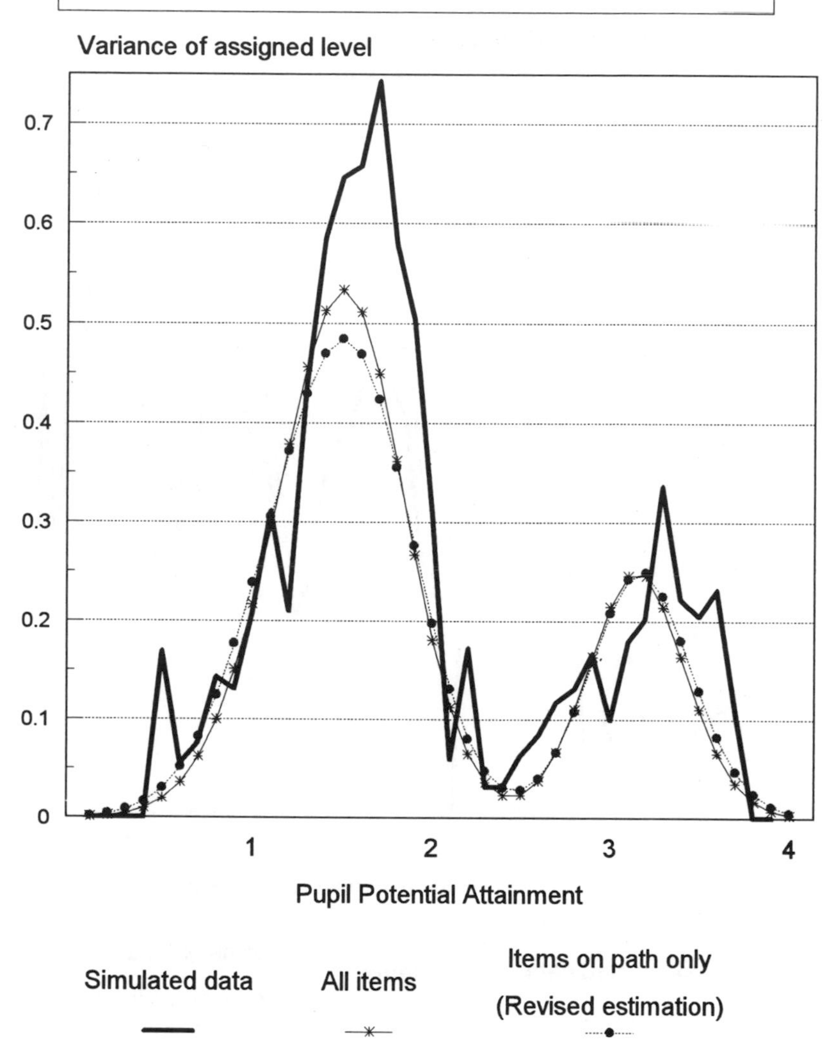

Figure 7

Attainment Target Structure D

Simulated data generated from Model U

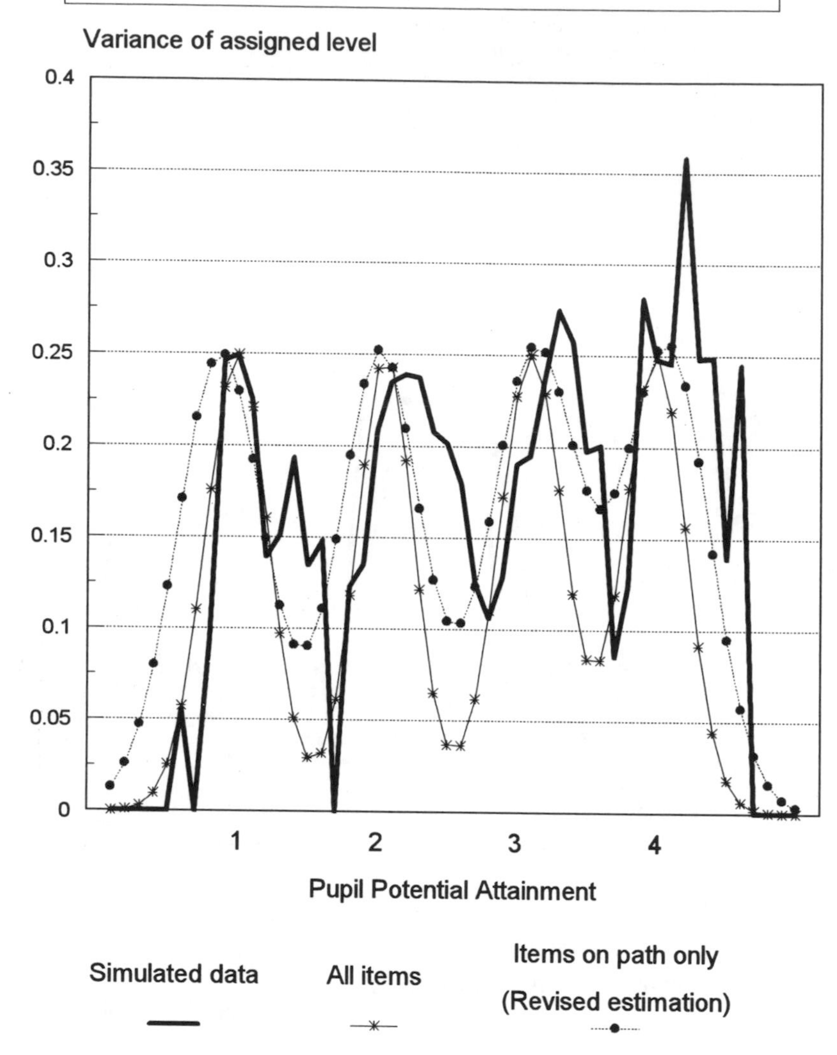

Figure 8

Attainment Target Structure C

Simulated data generated from Model LI

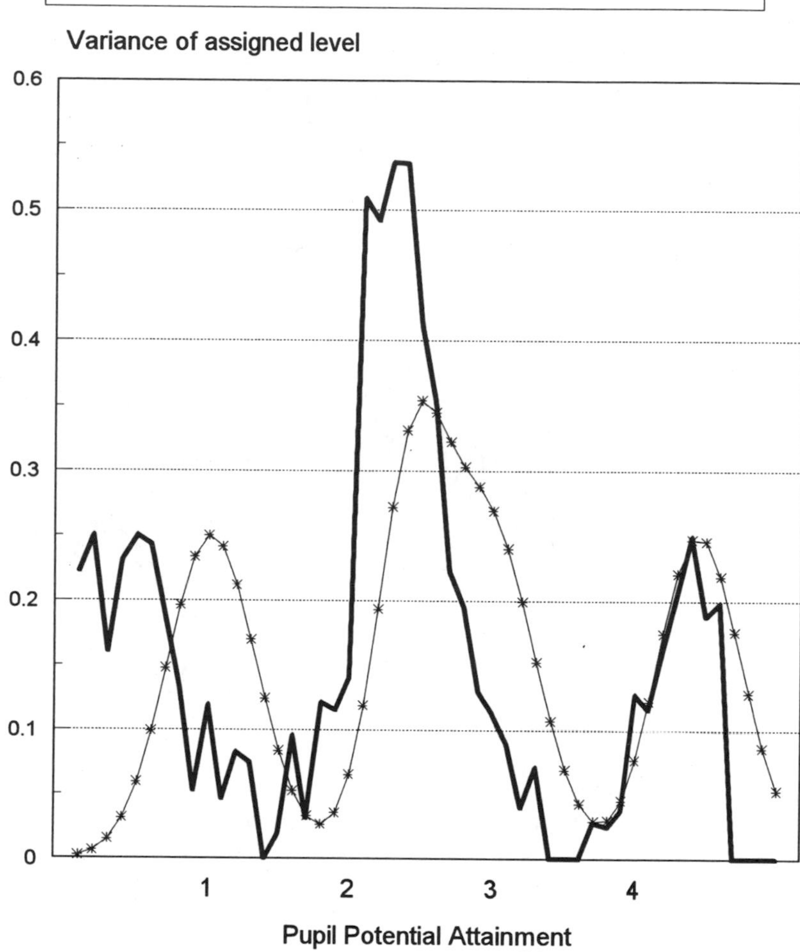

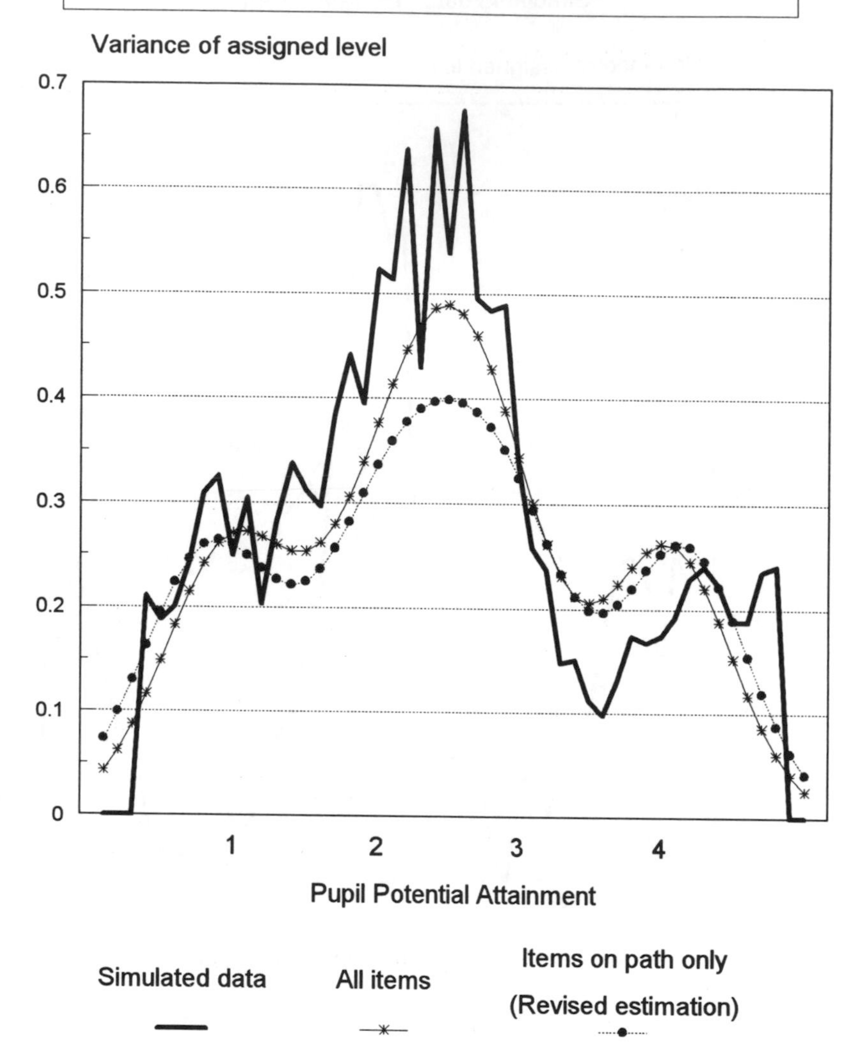
Figure 9
Attainment Target Structure D
Simulated data generated from Model LP
Variance of assigned level
0.7
0.6
0.5
0.4
0.3
0.2
0.1
0
1
2
3
4
Pupil Potential Attainment
Simulated data
All items
Items on path only
(Revised estimation)

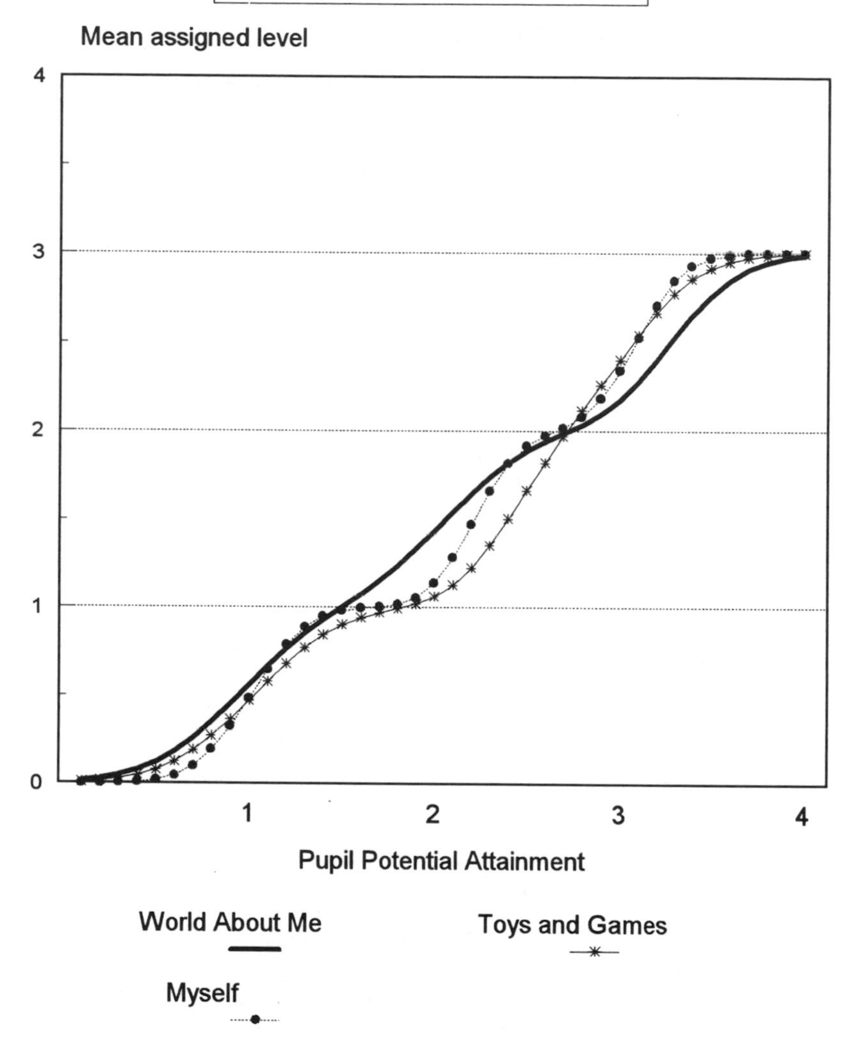
Figure 10
KS1 SAT Pilot 1990
Attainment Target Ma 3
Mean assigned level
4
3
2
1
0
1
2
3
4
Pupil Potential Attainment
World About Me
Toys and Games
Myself

Figure 11

KS1 SAT Pilot 1990 - Toys and Games

Attainment Target Ma 3

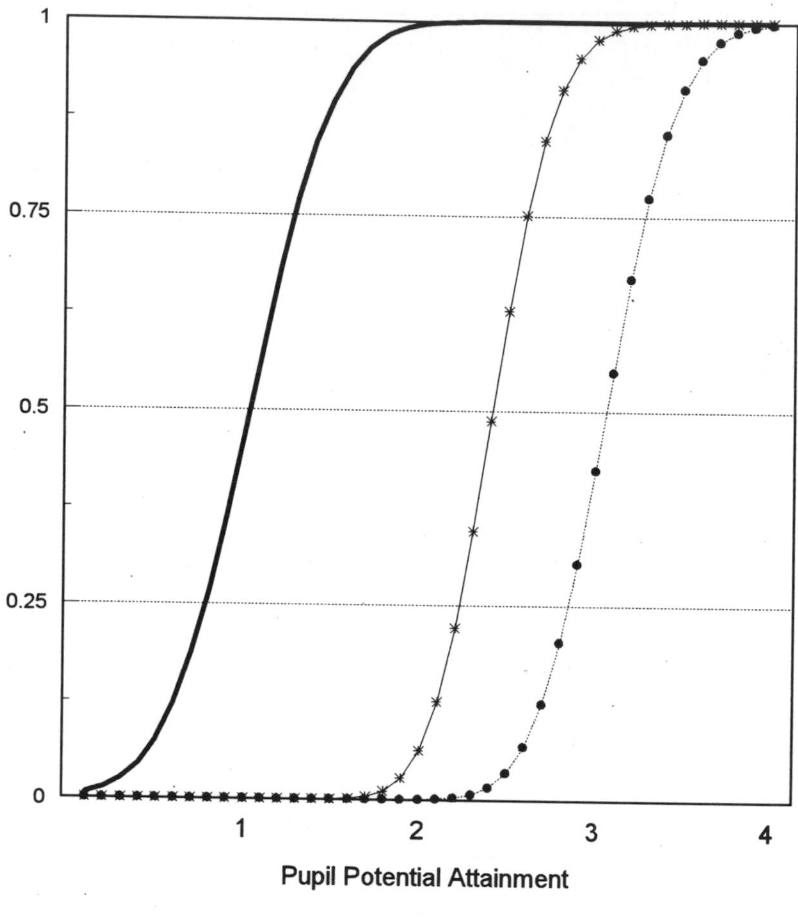

CHAPTER 7

MODELLING ADAPTIVE ASSESSMENT AT KEY STAGE 1

Dougal Hutchison
National Foundation for Educational Research

The Structure Of National Curriculum Assessment In England In Wales

Adaptive Key Stage 1 Assessment

The structure and history of National Curriculum Assessment are described elsewhere in this book (see Chapter 1). As a prelude to this chapter, however, it is important to emphasise the special features of Key Stage 1 assessment, particularly from 1991 on. Pilot 7-Year standard assessment tasks administered in 1990 were heavily criticised because of the time they took to administer, especially since this had to be done with small subgroups of the class, with the consequent problems of supervising the remainder. From 1991 Key Stage 1 standard assessment tasks were recast in an adaptive format in which the pupil started at one of a number of entry points, selected by the teacher. (In 1991 there were three, corresponding to the three possible Levels of teacher assessment.) The pupil's path through the standard assessment task was guided by the teacher on the basis of their performance so far. Figure 1 shows a summarised example of the paths through the standard attainment task.

Reliability measures in the psychometric literature

Problems

The standard reliability measures, such as described in Lord and Novick (1968), are not appropriate for use in this type of situation, and indeed Pollitt, in another paper in this volume, casts serious doubts upon their value as means of assessing tests at all. Schagen and Hutchison (1991) list basic ways in which National Curriculum Assessment (NCA) at Key Stage 1 differs from the usual norm-referenced testing (NRT) upon which much test theory is based:

a) The National Curriculum Assessments are devised to be criterion-referenced, rather than norm-referenced, identifying what a pupil can do, rather than how he or she fares compared with peers.
b) The tests are aimed to allocate children into ten assessment levels in a range of subjects. Within subjects, pupils are to be assessed on attainment targets (ATs).
c) To enable these allocations, the nature and level of achievement required for levels of each AT have been specified in terms of statements of attainment (SoAs).
d) The National Curriculum assessments are to be awarded on the basis of a combination of teacher assessment (TA) made throughout the year, and standard assessment tasks administered by the teacher.
e) The standard assessment tasks at Key Stage 1 were aimed to provide high validity in that they mimic the standard classroom learning situation and also provide evidence for the assessment over a variety of situations and contexts, ranging from written work by pupils to teacher observation. Moderation of the teachers' assessment, either of the TA or of the standard assessment task, is relatively light, and indeed would prove difficult in the case of those elements based on teacher observation.
f) The final assessments are to be a combination of TA and standard assessment task results, the latter in general (but with a few exceptions) taking precedence over the TA.
g) Pressure on teaching time means that the standard assessment tasks are unable to give the breadth and depth of coverage that would ideally be required of all aspects of all levels of all subjects.
h) The standard assessment tasks provide a number of elements, which together provide one or more assessments of a pupil's mastery of an SoA. Rules have been specified for aggregating pupil's scores from element to SoA, from SoA to AT, and from AT to subject. These rules are designed to be simple for a teacher to apply, and do not fit readily into normal statistical procedures. Schagen and Hutchison (op. cit.) show that these methods gave rise to aggregation problems with the previous version of the NCA.

While some of the public examination procedures in this country, in particular the GCSE, have departed substantially from the standardised formally administered multiple choice format, the NCA procedures represent a further departure, particularly in the use of lightly moderated teacher observation, and in the criterion-referenced perspective adopted, with its consequent innovative scoring and aggregation rules.

Modelling National Curriculum Assessment: previous research

Schagen and Hutchison (1991) show that conventional reliability coefficients are inappropriate for this type of assessment and argue that single-figure summaries are insufficiently informative, for two main reasons: firstly because performance of the estimator varies with the ability of the respondent; and secondly because the traditional reliabilities carry an implicit assumption that the result is unbiased while in fact the aggregation method itself is biased, giving lower results with increasing numbers of assessments aggregated. They argued that a modelling approach was an essential component of the development procedure, to see how the item facilities, dimensionality and scoring system of the task interacted in producing the final result. They suggested a number of graphical presentations which showed the performance and distribution of assessed responses at any given ability level.

There are substantial similarities between the 1991 and subsequent Key Stage 1 (KS1) assessment practices and that for 1990, for example the criterion-referenced assessment framework, the role of the teacher-administered standard assessment task, and the use of the statements of attainment for levels. There are also substantial differences, in particular the adaptive nature of the testing, the role of the initial teacher assessment, and the constrained choice (optional) sections. These differences meant that extensive theoretical and applied development was required before assessing the psychometric properties of the post-1991 standard assessment tasks.

Relevant aspects of previous research on adaptive testing

Thissen and Mislevy (1991) argue that adaptive testing is most usefully conceptualised in terms of an algorithm consisting of three parts:

1. How to START.
2. How to CONTINUE.
3. How to STOP.

In general, because of the complexity of the procedures used as CONTINUE and STOP rules, examples of adaptive testing are computer-administered. The psychometric properties of the NCA procedures are of particular interest, since they are not computer-administered or scored.

Three main approaches to the assessment of reliability under CAT have been used:

a) Replication of parallel tests. Lunz *et al.* (1990) have carried out this by giving original and replication tests together without making this explicit to the examinees. Some problems were encountered because of the variability in number of items used. Some borderline examinees were administered so many items that they virtually exhausted the item bank (as well as exhausting themselves!).
b) Using IRT and computer simulation (Bejar *et al.*, 1977).
c) Comparing with the results of a full administration, for example of a pencil and paper test (Weiss and Betz, 1973).

Generally it was found that CAT gives comparable precision using substantially fewer items, though estimates of the reduction vary. It is frequently found that the saving in time saved is less proportionately than in the number of items; it is suggested that this is mainly because items selected are the 'cutting edge' as far as each examinee is concerned, and thus take more time. Some studies of adaptive testing have shown higher correlations with underlying ability or validities against external criteria. Adaptive testing is likely to yield more nearly constant precision than standard tests throughout the range of abilities.

Modelling the assessment

Features of KS1 NCA from 1991 onwards

From 1991 Key Stage 1 standard assessment tasks were recast in an adaptive format in which the child's path through was to be guided by the teacher on the basis of their performance so far. The procedure can be summarised according to the Thissen and Mislevy algorithm quoted earlier as follows:

1. START by using the Teacher Assessment of the Level as indicating the starting level.
2. CONTINUE by testing at a higher (lower) Level if the pupil passes (fails) at that Level.

3. STOP if the pupil passes (fails) at the highest (lowest) Level OR if rule 2 (CONTINUE) would lead to reapplying the same assessment as one at an earlier stage.

The Level awarded is then determined by the teacher using instructions which are supplied with the assessment material.

The topics to be investigated.

In this paper we embark upon a modelling approach to NCA, and describe investigations of the following questions:

a) Modelling requires estimates of item facilities, or allied properties. How do we estimate these, given that only a subset of the population, and not a random one at that, is faced with the items?
b) To what extent is it legitimate to assume unidimensionality in modelling? This and the previous question are closely interrelated, since some of the potential methods of imputing facilities rely on the assumption of unidimensionality. (In this paper, we only assess the effect to which a unidimensional model provides a reasonable description of the data; we do not here investigate the effect of departures from unidimensionality.)
c) What is the effect of the teacher entry point? For example, what happens if the pupil is entered at the wrong Level — can the adaptive aspects of the assessment cope with it? Or, for example, could a teacher improve their pupils' performance by deliberately entering them for too high a Level?
d) How much time does the adaptive testing actually save?

In the next two sections, we consider procedures for handling missing data, and investigate whether a single dimensional model is likely to provide a satisfactory representation of the process for modelling purposes. We describe these topics separately, for clarity, though the actual process of developing the modelling was more a zigzag path between the two, than two distinct stages.

Imputation and missing data

Nature of the missing data

In the results from the administration of the standard tasks, a substantial proportion of the data for any pupil for any item is missing. Thus, for example, out of 5,345 pupils in total, the numbers with responses on the elements of Ma1 varied from 2,326 (43.5 per cent) to 4,429 (82.9 per cent), and on En2 responses varied from 1,771 (33 per cent) to 4136 (77.4 per cent). These results are not by any means missing at random however: they are designed to be missing, since a substantial shortening of the test was achieved by routeing pupils away from taking items where it was considered that this would add nothing to the determination of the Level the pupil attained. If a pupil had already failed more than one item in an AT at a Level, and thus failed the Level anyway whatever their performance on the remaining items, nothing would be gained as far as determining the Level was concerned by putting the pupil through any remaining assessments for the AT at that Level. Similarly, where a pupil had already passed a Level, there would be no point in administering the Level below, since the Level awarded was the highest Level attained, and thus the results at the lower one were not relevant to the determination of the Level. (It is possible that the results might be of some interest in the classroom to the class teacher.)

Another type of inference could be made from a pupil not having taken a Level: if a pupil had attempted and passed Level 2, then it could be inferred that missing results at Level 1 implied that the pupil could do Level 1 and would have passed any Level 1 items had they been presented. Similarly for a pupil failing Level 1, it could be inferred that missing results at Level 3 could be equated with not passing. Because of the separation of the Levels, so that one Level is intended to represent two years' educational progress, this is, on the face of it, a reasonable assumption (though see Christie, this volume).

Imputing for missing data: stage 1— Procrustean Imputation

We imputed for some of the missing data, using the following algorithm which took into account the eventual level determined for the pupil using the official aggregation rule. If items are missing at

Level 1	if Pupil Level is 2 or above,	missing = pass
Level 2	if Pupil Level is 1 or below,	missing = fail
	if Pupil Level is 3,	missing = pass
Level 3	if Pupil Level is 2 or below,	missing = fail.

We did not attempt to impute for missing items at the Level actually awarded, since these could arise for a number of reasons.

The effect of this imputation procedure on the proportion of missing items is given below.

Table 1: Proportion of data missing

	Un-imputed	Partially imputed
Maths	.69	.51
English	.35	.11
Science	.57	.41

The position after imputation is actually healthier than appears, since not all of the mathematics targets or the science targets are compulsory. Children have to be assessed on **one** of

Ma5
Ma8
Ma10
Ma13

and **one** of

Sc3
Sc5
Sc6. (NFER/BGC, 1991).

The figures for English are thus a better indication of the situation than are those for Mathematics and Science. (See Appendix for the meanings of the targets).

This imputation procedure may however be somewhat arbitrary, since it is not absolutely certain that a pupil failing one Level will **necessarily** fail all the items on a higher Level. While the average difference between the Levels is aimed to correspond to two years of academic progress, the differences in particular ATs may be larger or smaller than this, and particular items may even overlap in difficulty with items at another Level (see Hutchison and Schagen, 1991). If a particular item were substantially too easy for its nominal Level, then pupils at a lower Level might well pass it, were they to be given the opportunity to take it. Similarly an item that was too difficult for its Level might well pose problems to pupils at a higher Level, and not all might pass it if they were to take it. Also, it happens that pupils will fail relatively simple items through inattention, carelessness or a gap in their knowledge. For this reason it seems that this imputation procedure may be rather too arbitrary, and we now go on to investigate a further stage of imputation. We refer to this first stage of the imputation as **Procrustean Imputation,** to emphasise its arbitrary nature, and the way in which items were chopped off 'at the head' as being too difficult, and 'at the feet' as being too easy.

IRT Imputation

In this next imputation procedure, we fit a statistical model to the responses, giving values for item difficulties and for person potential performance. We then impute results for the missing item responses. Obviously no information on potential performance is available for those with no responses at all, and these are omitted. For convenience, and because of the commercial availability of widely used and tested computer packages, we use the IRT approach (see Lord, 1980). We fitted a two-parameter logistic model

$$p_{ij} = 1 / [1 + \exp\{-a_i(\Theta_j - b_i)\}]$$

for the probability of a correct response from the jth pupil to the ith item. b_i represents the item difficulty, Θ_j the pupil potential attainment, and a_i is a discrimination parameter measuring the 'sharpness' with which the item distinguishes between those who can pass it and those who cannot. We chose to fit a two-parameter model, rather than a one-parameter or a three-parameter, because there is a small but consistent improvement in fitting the 2-parameter model rather than the one-parameter (Schagen and Hutchison, 1991), and because the third parameter in the three-parameter model is sometimes conceptualised as a 'guessing' parameter, especially for multiple-choice models, while it must be questionable whether such a parameter will have any relevance in our application.

The procedure was as follows:

a) Item parameters and individual potential attainments were estimated using the program BILOG. Each AT was calibrated independently. The Procrustean-imputed data was used as a starting point.

b) Individual potential attainments and item parameters were merged with the original results. Where an item was missing it was imputed by a drawing of a [1,0] score according to the model.
Where all items were missing for a case on that AT, then that case was dropped for that AT.

c) The process (steps a) and b)) was repeated. It could have been further iterated to a specified degree of consistency, but in practice facilities had settled down with very few discrepancies by this stage.

Tables 2 - 4 compare the original unadjusted facilities with those resulting from our original arbitrary imputation, and from the IRT imputations. The first column shows the original 'raw' facilities, calculated by dividing the number getting an item right by the number actually taking it, as well as the actual number taking it. The second column shows the results of Procrustean imputation. The last two columns show the results of two iterations of the IRT imputation procedure described above for ATs Ma1, Sc1 and En2. For the remaining ATs assessed, only one IRT imputation is shown, since little is gained by the second imputation.

Thus, looking at Table 2, dealing with Ma1, we see that under half (2,366 of 5,345) pupils actually provided a response to AT 1a. Of these, 96 per cent got it correct. Though this is not directly observable from the table, the reason for the small response is that many Level 2 or Level 3 pupils will not have had to take it. Procrustean imputation provides a value for the majority of those missing, so that 4,802 now have a response, and 98 per cent of these got it correct. The first and second IRT imputations provide a small proportion of additional 'respondents', making the total up to 4,880, but not altering the facility. The remaining 465 cases had no response recorded on any of the SoAs in Ma1. The second IRT iteration does not alter the picture either. Thus in this example the Procrustean imputation has little effect on the overall facility, though substantially improving the number of responses, and the two IRT imputations have minimal effect, and would probably be scarcely worth carrying out.

On the other hand, the picture is quite different at the other end of the difficulty scale. A comparable proportion of pupils (2,326 out of 5,345) provided a response to SoA 3c, with a facility of .52. Procrustean imputation gives a higher number of responses of 4,678, as well as a much lower facility of .26. The first IRT iteration again increases the overall number again to 4,880, and brings the facility back up to .31; the second IRT iteration does not make any further difference. Thus we can say as an overall summary that the high-facility items are hardly affected by the imputation procedure, but that there is more effect on the lower-facility ones. The Procrustean imputations, as would be expected, are more extreme than are the unimputed results, since the additional pseudo-cases arising from the imputations are either certain yes's or certain no's. The first IRT iteration converts some of these certainties to probabilities, albeit high ones in many instances, so the estimated facilities are somewhat less extreme, and the second iteration differs little, if at all, from the first.

The pattern is comparable for the other ATs shown in the two following tables, with high facilities affected less than low ones, and the Procrustean imputation being more extreme than any of the others, except that the differences between the three imputations are larger.

We should make two comments at this point. First, we could have raised the numbers of cases and pseudo-cases combined still higher by fitting a model to the entire subject, for example for the combined items of Ma1, Ma3, Ma5, Ma8, Ma10 and Ma13, the total number of respondents to which is 5,030. This seems unsatisfactory for two reasons:

> a) it does not seem sound practice to impute for an AT for which we have no data at all (!);
> b) the assumption of a unidimensional model is less easy to maintain when we are dealing with different ATs (though presumably a two-dimensional model could be used).

Secondly, other studies, for example NAEP (Beaton and Johnson, 1987) have used the method of multiple imputation (Rubin, 1978). This is a method of allowing for missing data which preserves the second moments as well as the first moments in the imputed data. First a prediction of the missing element is made. Then a number of drawings of values with a random term reflecting in pupil's score added on to the original prediction. The addition of this uncertainty due to the random term helps reproduce the value of the variance and covariances. In our example the basic predictor is the fitted probability, and the uncertainty is introduced by the drawing of a [0,1] value.

We now turn to consider the extent to which it is legitimate to use a unidimensional model in summarising and imputing the data for an AT. At this stage we confine ourselves to assessing the proportion of the trace of the correlation matrix 'explained' by factors, and assessing whether it seems reasonably high. We aim in the future to carry out fuller analyses which fit multiple-factor models and to assess the difference from a single-factor model.

The dimensionality of SAT data

Introduction

As indicated above, one question to be answered about National Curriculum Assessment data is the extent to which measurements on a given attainment target (AT) may be considered to be measurements of a single ability or continuum, or at least treated in this way, from a statistical point of view. If this is not the case, and there exists more than one strong component of attainment for an individual AT, then our models must become more complex, and it is not clear how much meaning can be associated with the term 'Level' for an AT.

Earlier (Schagen and Hutchison, 1991), we investigated this question for the pilot National Curriculum Assessments, and came to the conclusion that unidimensionality held as a working assumption, with the first latent root accounting for a minimum of about 60 per cent of the total number of items after imputation. The assumption needs to be examined again for the 1992 data, because the adaptive testing framework means that a high proportion of items are omitted by design. While this made life easier for teachers and pupils, it also made it more difficult for methodological analysts such as ourselves.

For 1992 for each pupil the data available to us for each AT consisted of :

> **The teacher assessment (TA);**
> **scores on the various items taken, plus a 'missing' indicator for those not taken.**

How many dimensions?

The program TESTFACT (Wilson *et al*, 1991) is designed to carry out categorical factor analysis on item response data, using a multidimensional IRT model. We therefore decided to use it to attempt to answer the question at the head of this section. Two sets of analyses were carried out, corresponding to different methods of handling missing data. In the first of these, missing data was simply declared as missing in the input to the program, and TESTFACT ignored these in computation of the results. In the second of these, missing data was imputed using Procrustean imputation: not all missing responses could be resolved using this approach, and where this was the case, data was simply left as missing in the input to the program. This type of data has a tendency to give rise to Heywood cases, and to counteract this, we followed the recommendations of the manual, and imposed the program default priors on the intercept and slope parameters.

Tables 5 (a) and (b) show the proportion of the trace of the correlation matrix accounted for by each of the first three factors, for unimputed and Procrustean-imputed data.

We see that, for both original and imputed data, the proportions in the ATs explained by the first factor are quite high, between 60 and 65 per cent for the original data, and of the order of 70 per cent for the imputed data. The proportions at subject level are substantially lower for science and maths, though less so for English. Except in English, the proportions are smaller when teacher assessment (TA) results are included.

The figures for the AT analyses are comparable with those quoted by the authors for the pilot study of National Assessment at Key Stage 1, though quite high in comparison with figures quoted for NAEP data (Zwick, 1987). Figures for the subject analyses are still rather higher than those quoted by Zwick, op. cit. We infer from this that, for the purpose of reliability modelling in this set of data, a unidimensional model is going to be a reasonable assumption for ATs. However for subjects, except possibly English, the use of models assuming unidimensionality would require more caution. In any event we are only interested in the situation for ATs here. Further analysis of the effect of dimensionality would be of interest, and we propose to do this elsewhere.

Modelling the data: the impact of adaptive assessment

The effect on the Level attained

It is generally claimed that adaptive testing gives higher precision for the same number of items or the same time, or equivalently, the same precision for fewer items or less time (Wainer, 1991). However, before we can look at this question, there is a prior consideration. Schagen and Hutchison (1991) showed that the within-pupil aggregation arrangements had a biasing effect on the resultant Level assessed, with larger numbers of assessment giving lower Levels. Before considering the variation or, comparably, the time, we should first consider whether the adaptive procedure introduces any further bias into the result.

For convenience we used an Item Response Theory method as outlined in a previous section. One hundred simulations were carried out for each respondent. Using the potential attainment for the respondent and the item parameters estimated using the two-parameter model, we produced a set of [0,1] responses for each of the items. These were used in two ways. First, they were used as the responses for a notional whole-test administration, and the resultant Level calculated. They were also used as 'shadow' results for an adaptive administration, and a path was steered through the task, taking the TA Level as the start point, steering a path through the parts and Levels of the task using the (same) results for the non-adaptive assessment.

To gain an estimate of the saving in time by using the adaptive approach, we took the 'suggested times' for parts of a task, given in the *Handbook of Guidance for the SAT: 1991 Key Stage 1.* Where the results of following the instructions meant quitting the section part-way through, we used a proportionate allocation of the time.

Table 8.1 shows the result of a simulation comparing the results of an adaptive administration with a non-adaptive (entire test) administration for each of the ATs in the 1991 standard assessment task. The table shows mean results, as well as proportion of results that do not agree between the two modes of administration. One facet of the table that springs to the eye is that there are no instances in which the adaptive testing gives a **higher** result than does the non-adaptive. This is obvious, on reflection. Discrepancies could in theory arise when a pupil is not assessed on difficult items that they would have passed, or on easy items that they would have failed. However the aggregation system is such that only the first of these will actually create a discrepancy: a higher-Level success will over-write a lower-Level lack of success.

The second facet that can be seen is that even for the situation in which the adaptive testing gives a lower result, the discrepancies are very small. Indeed, except for Ma10, they appear virtually non-existent. We see that, within the confines of this simulation, there is very little effect of the mode of administration (adaptive/non-adaptive) on the result. If the actual results are the same, then the variance of the results must also be the same. We now turn to the question of the amount of time spent administering the assessments.

Table 7 shows from simulations the mean time for the pupils to spend on the task for the adaptive assessment, compared with a notional whole-test administration. The time saved varies, but ranges generally between about a half and a quarter. (En5 (Handwriting) is not organised as an adaptive assessment). It should be noted that this finding relates only to the time that pupils spent on the tasks: the time saved by teachers might be rather less, since for an assessment in a group of four, the task would have to carry on even if two (say) of the pupils dropped out.

Conclusions and discussion

The attempt to model adaptive testing data has given rise to a number of new problems, the major one of which has been that not all of the pupils took all of the items. This is a particularly sensitive problem where, as here, we do not have results available from a pretest, and makes it difficult to estimate item parameters for the population, and to investigate the dimensionality of the data.

A number of methods of imputing results and item parameters, giving different results, are discussed here. Imputation procedures depend upon the dimensionality of the data, and vice versa, so there is potentially a degree of circularity in estimating both the dimensionality and the item parameters. However, it does seem that the data can be effectively described by a unidimensional model, and that useful information of the performance of the procedure can be obtained based on this. Further research might look at the impact of using a multidimensional model.

Based on our simulation results, we find that the adaptive procedure

a) gives results that are very close to a whole-test administration, and
b) does so taking substantially less of the pupils' time.

There has to be some caution in applying these results to the real-world situation, because the times are not based on the actual 'live' administration of the standard task, and do not allow for the fact that pupils will complete tasks at different rates, and because a simulation is only that, and is of necessity a simplification of reality, not taking account of the classroom dynamic of carrying out the task.

Acknowledgments

The work on this paper has been carried in connection with ESRC Grant R000234137. Substantial support has also been given by the NFER itself.

I am grateful to SEAC for allowing the use of data from the standard assessment task at Key Stage 1, and to the NFER Key Stage 1 team for help and encouragement. Opinions expressed in this paper remain those of the author alone.

Figure 1

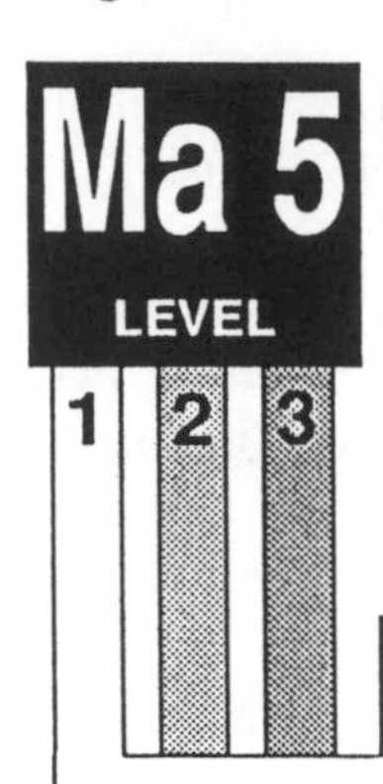

Ma 5 Handling Data

The activities given here cover a range of data handling, from simple sorting (at level 1) through to using a computer database (at level 4). They have been designed for use with large groups of children, unless otherwise stated.

Activity	Result	Outcome
Level 1 **30 minutes** **Sorting Ma 5/1a**	In total, fewer than two SoA achieved	Working towards level 1 (W)
	In total, two SoA achieved	**LEVEL 1** Go to level 2

Activity	Result	Outcome
Level 2 **50 minutes** **Part A:** **How Many Socks?** **Ma 5/2a** **Part B:** **How Many Vegetables?** **Ma 5/2b**	In total, fewer than two SoA achieved	If not previously attempted go to level 1
	In total, two SoA achieved	**LEVEL 2** Go to level 3

Activity	Result	Outcome
Level 3 **60 minutes** **Part A: The Bus Timetable** **Ma 5/3a** **Part B: Travelling Times** **Ma 5/3b** **Part C: Balloons in a Bag** **Ma 5/3c**	In total, fewer than two SoA achieved	If not previously attempted go to level 2
	In total, two SoA achieved	**LEVEL 3** You may wish to go to level 4
	In total, three SoA achieved	**LEVEL 3** Go to level 4

Table 2 (a): Unimputed and imputed facilities: Ma1

	Unimputed	Procrustean Imputation	IRT Imputation (N = 4880)	
			1st	2nd
1a	.96 (2366)	.98 (4802)	.98	.98
1b	.97 (2295)	.97 (4754)	.98	.98
1c	.99 (2356)	1.00 (4817)	1.00	1.00
2a	.95 (4429)	.87 (4863)	.89	.90
3a	.47 (4429)	.43 (4879)	.43	.43
2b	.91 (4227)	.81 (4773)	.81	.82
3b	.29 (4227)	.25 (4864)	.25	.25
2c	.90 (3952)	.80 (4664)	.81	.82
3c	.52 (2326)	.26 (4678)	.31	.31

Overall sample size 5345
Sample size with any recorded response to Ma1 4880

Table 2 (b): Unimputed and imputed facilities: Ma3-13

	Unimputed	Procrustean Imputation	IRT Imputation
Ma3			
1a	.97 (2553)	.98 (4449)	.98 (4840)
2a	.77 (4173)	.69 (4840)	.71
2c	.75 (3674)	.59 (4840)	.61
3a	.44 (2111)	.19 (4814)	.21
3b	.33 (1414)	.10 (4695)	.12
3c	.49 (1821)	.19 (4818)	.20
Ma5			
1a	.96 (610)	.98 (1171)	.97 (1221)
2a	.88 (993)	.77 (1221)	.80
2b	.85 (983)	.73 (1221)	.76
3a	.71 (673)	.39 (1221)	.57
3c	.51 (587)	.25 (1221)	.26
Ma8			
1a	.80 (138)	.91 (315)	.91 (324)
2a	.89 (264)	.81 (312)	.83
2b	.88 (269)	.81 (316)	.82
2c	.85 (245)	.75 (303)	.75
3a	.68 (136)	.29 (321)	.31
3b	.71 (153)	.34 (323)	.40
3c	.50 (147)	.23 (323)	.23
Ma10			
1a	.92 (1219)	.96 (2586)	.95 (2659)
1b	.95 (1249)	.98 (2602)	.96
2a	.88 (2166)	.83 (2659)	.84
2b	.75 (2015)	.67 (2659)	.69
3a	.65 (1635)	.40 (2659)	.44
Ma 13			
1a	.86 (382)	.94 (908)	.93 (956)
1b	.89 (409)	.95 (915)	.95
2a	.96 (880)	.90 (956)	.91
2b	.84 (829)	.75 (956)	.78
3a	.58 (506)	.30 (956)	.31
3b	.38 (416)	.16 (956)	.17

Table 3 (a): Unimputed and imputed facilities: Sc1

	Unimputed	Procrustean Imputation	IRT Imputation (N = 4885)	
			1st	2nd
1a	.97 (1901)	.99 (4664)	.99	.99
1b	.96 (1902)	.99 (4664)	.98	.98
2a	1.00 (4567)	.95 (4857)	.95	.95
3a	.75 (4567)	.72 (4858)	.71	.71
2b	.97 (4511)	.91 (4847)	.92	.92
3d	.61 (4511)	.57 (4854)	.57	.58
2c	.95 (4463)	.90 (4832)	.89	.89
2d	.93 (4359)	.87 (4761)	.87	.88
2e	.94 (4354)	.87 (4761)	.87	.88
3h	.46 (4354)	.41 (4833)	.42	.42
2f	.94 (4456)	.88 (4833)	.89	.89
3c	.46 (1792)	.18 (4744)	.21	.22
3e	.57 (2091)	.25 (4805)	.28	.29
3f	.77 (2132)	.34 (4856)	.39	.40
3i	.73 (1909)	.28 (4845)	.33	.35

Overall sample size 5345
Sample with any recorded response to Sc1 4858

Table 3 (b): Unimputed and imputed facilities: Sc3-Sc6

	Unimputed	Procrustean Imputation	IRT
Sc3			
1a	.97 (1675)	.98 (3288)	.98 (3333)
2b	.95 (2900)	.92 (3333)	.94
2c	.98 (2965)	.96 (3333)	.97
3a	.85 (2382)	.61 (3333)	.64
3b	.86 (2702)	.70 (3333)	.72
Sc5			
1a	.88 (289)	.94 (557)	.92 (588)
2a	.93 (527)	.86 (588)	.90
2b	.93 (494)	.80 (588)	.85
3a	.79 (428)	.58 (588)	.67
3b	.61 (311)	.33 (588)	.35
Sc6			
1a	.94 (392)	.98 (1029)	.98 (1046)
2a	.89 (870)	.82 (1031)	.82
2b	.93 (894)	.86 (1045)	.86
2c	.94 (860)	.85 (1030)	.87
3a	.81 (686)	.53 (1046)	.59
3b	.62 (725)	.43 (1046)	.44

Table 4 (a): Unimputed and imputed facilities: En2

	Unimputed	Procrustean	IRT Imputation (N = 4941)	
			1st	2nd
1a	.99 (1779)	.99 (4297)	.99	.99
1b	.97 (1771)	.99 (4292)	.99	.99
1c	.99 (1788)	1.00 (4307)	1.00	.99
1d	.97 (1763)	.99 (4284)	.98	.98
2a	.87 (3980)	.78 (4971)	.82	.83
2b	.89 (3826)	.73 (4941)	.78	.80
2c	.92 (3483)	.74 (4941)	.78	.79
2d	.94 (3477)	.75 (4941)	.79	.80
2e	.96 (4136)	.80 (4941)	.86	.87
3c	.57 (4136)	.47 (4941)	.49	.49
2f	.85 (3549)	.70 (4941)	.73	.74
3a	.58 (2320)	.27 (4941)	.32	.31
3	.74 (1970)	.30 (4941)	.34	.37
3d	.67 (1894)	.26 (4941)	.28	.29
3e	.74 (2667)	.40 (4941)	.47	.50
3f	.71 (1766)	.25 (4941)	.29	.31

Overall sample size 5345
Sample size with any recorded response to En2 4941

Table 4 (b): **Unimputed and imputed facilities: En3-En5**

	Unimputed	Procrustean Imputation	IRT Imputation
En3			
1a	.99 (4407)	.99 (4742)	.99 (4803)
2a	.58 (4407)	.57 (4470)	.58
3a	.22 (4407)	.20 (4801)	.21
2b	.92 (4395)	.84 (4792)	.86
3b	.18 (4395)	.17 (4800)	.17
2c	.88 (4265)	.79 (4757)	.81
3c	.22 (4265)	.20 (4802)	.20
3e	.34 (1511)	.11 (4620)	.16
En4			
1a	1.00 (2099)	1.00 (4610)	1.00 (4867)
1b	.96 (2023)	.98 (4561)	.98
1c	.99 (4702)	.99 (4779)	.99
2a	.91 (4702)	.90 (4843)	.90
2b	.86 (4272)	.76 (4835)	.78
3a	.21 (4272)	.18 (4866)	.18
2c	.71 (3754)	.60 (4454)	.63
3b	.24 (3754)	.18 (4845)	.19
2d	.89 (4222)	.79 (4780)	.82
3d	.28 (4222)	.25 (4843)	.25
En5			
1a	1.00 (4730)	1.00 (4730)	1.00 (4744)
2b	.84 (4730)	.84 (4744)	.84
3a	.04 (4730)	.04 (4744)	.04
2a	.87 (4128)	.77 (4744)	.80

Table 5 (a) Proportion of total explained by latent roots for various ATs: unimputed data

	N of items	Root 1	2	3
Mathematics	(38)	26.2	23.2	18.6
+ *TA*	(56)	23.1	16.5	13.8
Ma1 (c)	9	67.1	17.8	8.1
Ma3 (c)	6	69.2	13.8	6.6
Ma5	5	63.6	24.6	5.7
Ma8	7	62.0	26.1	6.9
Ma10	5	50.8	35.7	6.9
Ma13	6	58.8	33.3	5.0
Mean		61.9	25.2	6.5
Science	(31)	39.9	20.3	16.8
+ *TA*	(43)	28.4	18.9	16.8
Sc1 (c)	15	55.1	13.9	8.9
Sc3	5	61.2	22.4	12.6
Sc5	5	59.7	21.2	13.1
Sc6	6	70.6	9.7	8.8
Mean		61.7	16.8	10.9
English	(38)	52.4	13.9	7.2
+ *TA*	(50)	53.7	11.2	5.5
En2 (c)	16	55.6	23.9	9.1
En3 (c)	8	74.4	7.4	5.8
En4 (c)	10	63.6	15.3	7.4
En5 (c)	4	66.2	16.3	13.3
Mean		65.0	15.7	8.9
All	107	18.6	14.8	7.2

Note (1) 'Corrected' latent roots used
(2) (c) indicates compulsory attainment target

Table 5 (b) Proportion of total explained by latent roots for various ATs (Procrustean Imputation)

	N of items	Root 1	Root 2	Root 3
Mathematics	(38)	41.1	12.6	9.5
+ TA	(56)	30.6.	27.9	6.4
Ma1	9	77.1	11.0	6.4
Ma3	6	77.3	10.3	6.3
Ma5	5	71.6	19.6	4.5
Ma8	7	67.1	24.5	4.2
Ma10	5	68.3	23.9	4.0
Ma13	6	65.1	27.1	4.4
Mean		71.1	19.4	5.0
Science	(31)	46.1	25.3	11.8
+ TA	(43)	42.7	25.2	6.2
Sc1	15	68.1	16.6	4.3
Sc3	5	65.7	22.5	10.5
Sc5	5	67.3	16.9	10.2
Sc6	6	78.9	10.4	6.1
Mean		70.1	23.5	7.8
English	(38)	57.3	11.8	7.2
+ TA	(50)	57.3	9.6	6.9
En2	16	58.2	23.0	11.1
En3	8	73.8	11.5	6.0
En4	10	70.2	13.4	5.9
En5	4	69.7	13.7	13.1
Mean		68.0	15.4	4.1
All	107	23.7	19.8	9.7

Note (1) 'Corrected' latent roots used
(2) (c) indicates compulsory attainment target

Table 6: Mean level achieved: adaptive and non-adaptive testing: model results.

AT	'Adaptive' (a)	'Non-adaptive' (b)	Proportion a) too low	Proportion a) too high
Maths				
Ma1	2.12	2.12	<.01	0
Ma3	1.70	1.70	.00	0
Ma5	1.09	1.91	<.01	0
Ma8	2.07	2.08	<.01	0
Ma10	2.12	2.15	.02	0
Ma13	1.99	2.00	<.01	0
Science				
Sc1	2.08	2.08	<.01	0
Sc3	2.53	2.54	<.01	0
Sc5	1.96	1.98	<.01	0
Sc6	2.29	2.29	<.01	0
English				
En2	1.69	1.69	<.01	0
En3	1.63	1.63	.00	0
En4	1.93	1.93	.00	0
En5	1.81	.81	.00	0

Table 7 **Mean total time taken: adaptive and non-adaptive testing: model results.**

AT	'Adaptive' Time	'Non-adaptive' Time
Maths		
Ma1	43.2	75.0
Ma3	43.1	72.0
Ma5	49.3	70.0
Ma8	66.5	90.0
Ma10	41.9	60.0
Ma13	50.6	70.0
Science		
Sc1	55.1	75.0
Sc3	42.0	70.0
Sc5	48.3	70.0
Sc6	41.1	65.0
English		
En2	48.2	95.0

REFERENCES

BEATON, A. AND JOHNSON, E. (1989). 'The Average Response Method (ARM) method of scaling' in: Beaton, A (Ed) *Implementing the New Design: the NAEP 1983-84 Technical Report.* Princeton, NJ: ETS.

BEJAR, I. I. WEISS, D. J. and GIALLUCA, K. A. (1977). *An Information Comparison of Conventional and Adaptive Tests in the Measurement of Classroom Achievement.* Research Report 77-7, Psychometric Methods Program, Department, University of Minnesota, Minneapolis MN 55455

DES and WELSH OFFICE (1987). *National Curriculum: Task Group on Achievement and Testing — A Report* (the TGAT Report). London: HMSO.

GREAT BRITAIN STATUTORY INSTRUMENTS (1990). *Education (National Curriculum) (Assessment Arrangements for English, Mathematics and Science)* Order 1990.

LORD, F. M. (1980). *Applications of Item Response Theory to Practical Testing Problems.* Hillsdale, NJ: Lawrence Erlbaum Associates.

LORD, F. M. AND NOVICK, M. (1968). *Statistical Theories of Mental Test Scores.* Reading, Mass: Addison-Wesley.

LUNZ, M. E., BERGSTROM, B. A., and GERSHON, R. (1990). 'Test-Retest Consistency of Computer Adaptive Tests.' Paper presented at the National Council on Measurement in Education, Boston MA, April 1990.

NFER/BGC CONSORTIUM (1991). *Handbook of Guidance for the SAT.* Windsor: NFER-NELSON.

RUBIN, D. (1978). 'Multiple imputation in sample surveys', *Proceedings of the Survey Research Methods Section of the American Statistical Association*, 20-34.

SCHAGEN, I. and HUTCHISON, D. (1991). Reliability and Allied Measurements for Criterion-Referenced Assessment. Final Report to the ESRC, December 1991.

THISSEN, D. and MISLEVY, R. (1991). 'Testing Algorithms.' in WAINER (Ed) *Computerised Adaptive Testing: a primer.* Hillsdale, NJ: Lawrence Erlbaum Associates.

WEISS, D. J. (Ed) (1983). *New horizons in Testing: Latent Trait Test Theory and Computerised Adaptive Testing.* Academic Press, New York and London.

WEISS, D. J. and BETZ, N.E. (1973). *Ability Measurement: Conventional or Adaptive?* Research Report, **73** 1, Mineapolis: University of Minnesota, Department of Pschology, Psychometric Methods Program, 1973.

WILSON, D. WOOD, R. and GIBBONS, R. (1991). *TESTFACT: Test Scoring, Item Statistics, and Item Factor Analysis: 1991 Edition.* (Compute Program). Mooresville: Scientific Software, Inc.

ZWICK, R. (1987) 'Assessment of the dimensionality of Year 15 reading data' in: BEATON, A (Ed) *Implementing the New Design : the NAEP 1983-84 Technical Report.* Princeton, NJ: ETS.

Appendix: Attainment targets assessed in the 1991 standard assessment task

Mathematics

Ma1	Using and applying mathematics
Ma3	Number
Ma5	Number/Algebra
Ma8	Measures

Science

Sc1	Exploration of science
Sc3	Processes of life
Sc5	Human influences on the earth
Sc6	Types and uses of materials

English

En2	Reading
En3	Writing
En4	Spelling
En5	Handwriting

CHAPTER 8
DISCUSSANTS' COMMENTS

Caroline Gipps
University of London Institute of Education

First paper:
'Reconceptualising Validity, Dependability and Reliability for National Curriculum Assessment' given by Dylan Wiliam

Much of this paper deals with existing definitions of validity and reliability, and is useful in showing how notions of validity have shifted over the years. Overall, though, it is reliability which is more widely being pursued in developing assessments than validity.

There is no doubt that the whole area of validity and reliability needs rethinking, particularly in relation to criterion-referenced assessment, authentic performance-based assessment, and teacher assessment, all of which are key components of National Curriculum Assessment. The problem is that the legacy of psychometrics with the standardisation of assessment paramount in order to promote reliability has led to, in the USA certainly, tests that are so standardised and 'objective' that they are in an educational sense, pretty worthless. Now, with an approach based on educational assessment, rather than psychometric assessment, employing approaches linked more to criterion-referencing, the underlying assumptions are different. For example, we are not looking for a spread of scores as in a normal distribution, conditions are not fully standardised and, with lengthy assessment, we cannot have a large number of tasks sampling across the domain. Dylan is, therefore, quite right to be attempting to reconceptualise reliability and validity. I like the term dependability which he describes as a combination of content validity and reliability. A paper by Harlen in another symposium at this conference defines dependability as 'maximising reliability to a level appropriate for the use of the test whilst maintaining high levels of validity'. Dylan's use of the term dependability as a combination of content validity and reliability does not however include the consequences of test use, which has now become an important element of the theory of validity.

The focus in validity on the consequence of use, which in a National Curriculum Assessment setting will include the impact of league tables, will make construct and content validity even more important, since we will have to think about what we are assessing in relation to what we wish to see taught. In relation to Dylan's definition, that a valid test is one you would like teachers to teach toward, this is fine as far as it goes and enhances very well the notion of conseqential validity, but this on its own is not cnough, sincc thc tcst may still have construct under-representation; we need to ascertain not just that the test is one we would like teachers to teach towards, but that it covers the whole of the domain which we are interested in assessing.

Second paper:

'The Reliability of National Curriculum Assessment at Key Stages 1 and 2', given by Diane Shorrocks and Nick Nelson

Shorrocks and Nelson's paper describes their work evaluating the Key Stage 1 assessments in 1991. Comparing teacher assessment scores and SAT scores with their own specially devised assessments is a very neat way to go about analysing the dependability of these different assessments. In essence what this team was doing was evaluating the reliability of the mastery classifications across the three sorts of assessment in relation to assigning children to the Levels 1, 2 and 3 of the National Curriculum in the attainment targets. As we know, the comparison among TA, SAT and ENCA in 1991 was disturbingly low. The authors point to a number of reasons why this might be so, including that the assessments were carried out by different people at different points in time. To this we must add that they were quite different assessment tasks, and different types of assessment, although the assessment criteria were common. The burgeoning literature on performance assessment and authentic assessment in the USA, and evidence from the Assessment of Performance Unit, tells us quite clearly that performance is highly task-specific, and we know in any case that performance, even on 'objective' tests, is highly context-dependent. So we know that we are fairly unlikely to get high levels of consistency across different types of assessment, even when using the same assessment criteria. That levels of agreement were higher in 1992 is, of course, partly due to teachers becoming more used to the assessments and statements of attainments; but I feel it is important to add that because the teachers did not have to do their teacher assessment until after the SATs had been completed that year, that the higher level of agreement may be because the teachers' assessments were not actually made, simply recorded after the SAT and thus reflect the SAT score. Evidence from our research study of KS1 teachers indicates that indeed it was widespread practice for the teachers not to make teacher assessments in 1992 until after the SAT.

I particularly like Shorrocks' point about the nature of the domain being assessed, and how this should determine the appropriate model for sampling items from it (whether a random approach is taken, or one in relation to a hierarchy of progression). This emphasises that we must keep going back to the domain we are assessing, and check that what we are doing in assessment design and analysis is logically appropriate. In essence this is a plea for an extension of construct validity.

In SAT-type activities the tension is between the number of items and manageability, as this paper points out. In order to be able to generalise, even within the domain, never mind outside the domain, we need large numbers of items, which in performance assessment terms is likely to be unmanageable. One can argue for this amount of assessment on the grounds that if the assessment tasks are good, then this is time well spent for the student; unfortunately there is a problem with public acceptability here, or indeed political acceptability, as was found with the extended tasks for KS3 English and Maths in the early stages of national assessment development.

Third paper:

'Teacher Assessment: A Sociological Perspective', given by Ann Filer

I found this paper most interesting, although I do not agree with Filer's analysis of the 'push' for 'objectivity' in teacher assessment by various agencies and the Government. I do not think that at any point has the Government wanted teacher assessment to be seen as an objective assessment. There is concern over comparability, certainly, but few believe that TA can ever be 'objective', particularly in this post-modern age. There are many people, not just those on the Right, who view teacher assessment with suspicion for anything other than very informal purposes.

The importance of Filer's paper, I think, is that it shows how unrealistic it is to think in terms of objective teacher assessment. However, this does not mean that we should abandon it; what we must do, in the name of equity and fairness, is to tie teacher assessment to assessment criteria, provide training in observation and questioning, and offer group moderation to get some consistency, at least, within and across schools. This would also help to limit teacher stereotyping tendencies in assessment, which have such a worrying role to play in the process of social differentiation.

Conclusions

My main point is that we must acknowledge the differences between highly standardised testing procedures, performance-based tasks assessed in the classroom or outside it, and teacher assessment, all of which play a part in National Curriculum Assessment. If we push teacher assessment and performance assessment too closely towards standardisation, in order to satisfy traditional reliability, we are in danger of throwing out the baby with the bathwater. The worksheet 'Science Tasks' for the SATs at KS1 in 1993 are a prime example of how trying to turn something that should be performance-based into a highly standardised procedure simply results in bad tests. Assessment is not an exact science, and it is the legacy of psychometrics to make us believe that it is. As our symposium on quality in assesssment at this conference is trying to get over, we must move to other ways of looking at how we can offer quality assurance for assessment. The other thing that we know, and psychometrics ignores, is that pupil performance is highly task- and context-dependent, and generally unpredictable. We know this from work in psychology and learning theory. To continue to assume that we can measure pupils' performance accurately and precisely with high levels of reliability and replicability, particularly in complex tasks, is to delude both ourselves and others.

So I welcome the message of the three papers in the first half of this symposium, and my view echoes that of Nick Nelson's throwaway line, that we may need to abandon traditional notions of reliability; I believe that we may need, for school-based assessment anyway, to move beyond reliability and standardisation completely. What we actually need to do, rather than to tinker with different statistical approaches, is to re-conceptualise what we mean by quality in assessment; in other words, we need other ways of warranting assessment-based conclusions. The reason that we are having to reconceptualise some of these issues within National Curriculum Assessment, is because assessment is undergoing a paradigm shift. We are in the process of shifting from a scientific psychometric paradigm to a paradigm of educational assessment, whose conception of performance is quite different. This mirrors the shift in educational evaluation from the experimental paradigm to more qualitative, naturalistic approaches. For example, it may be that instead of generalisability we focus on transferability: since performance is context-bound, we could specify the context in which a particular achievement has been demonstrated, and then judge whether this will be transferable to other contexts; we offer more description of contexts, and we then allow the user to make decisions about whether the performance observed in the assessment will relate to the context in which the user is interested. With very complex constructs, we may be better to credit a specific complex accomplishment in and of itself, without the burden of generalising to or beyond the domain, as we do in higher education with the examination of dissertations. We also need to have a common understanding of criteria; this can be achieved through training of teachers, and through moderation approaches. It is important to have consistency of approach to the assessment, partly so that the assessment across teachers is comparable, but also so that we know teachers are assessing the same construct. Again, this relies on training and moderation. I believe there are a number of ways of reconceptualising reliability in order to offer consistency across assessments and we need to address this as a priority.

Rob Taylor, Evaluation and Monitoring Unit,
School Examinations and Assessment Council

Papers by Schagen, Hutchison and Pollitt

All involved in the development, implementation and monitoring of National Curriculum Assessment have been concerned with the reliability of the assessments made. Indeed, some would argue that there has been an unhealthy obsession with reliability at the expense of legitimate concerns about the validity of assessment.

Nevertheless, it is clearly important in the context of a high-stakes public assessment system that all those involved with the system have some understanding of the reliability that can be attributed to the information which the system produces. Much of the debate over the past few years has concentrated on the appropriateness of the various statistical models that can be used to estimate test reliability. It is well understood that models derived for use with norm-referenced tests make assumptions that may not hold in the context of criterion-referenced tests. Some of the innovative work being carried out in the context of National Curriculum Assessment test development is evidence of the steps that are being taken to develop a more appropriate model of test reliability. The research being carried out by the NFER, and represented by the papers presented by Ian Schagen on graphical representation of the reliability of National Curriculum Assessment and Dougal Hutchison on modelling adaptive assessment at Key Stage 1, is testament to that work. There is little doubt that their research will repay careful consideration by those charged with developing tests in the future. The models they are developing represent potentially powerful diagnostic tools for test developers and evaluators.

During the debate about reliability it has been too easy to forget the needs of the users of performance data. There sometimes appears to be an assumption made that the needs of all users are the same, and that therefore a single solution should be sought to the problems of measuring and describing reliability

A simple, but real analogy should be sufficient to point out the multiple needs of users. British Rail, under the auspices of the Citizens' Charter, is required to measure and publish information about the reliability of its services. This is an easy task in a technical sense. The reliability of a particular service is a function of its expected and observed departure and arrival times. A single measure can be used to describe the reliability of 0757 from Bath Spa to Paddington. The needs of passengers travelling on that particular service however vary considerably. A passenger needing to be at a particular meeting at a certain time interprets and uses the reliability statistic in a very different way from one who needs to reach London, but has no set deadlines to meet. Similarly, a passenger deciding whether to purchase an annual season ticket will view the reliability figures very differently from one who is buying a one-off ticket for recreational travel.

The analogy can be extended into the educational sphere. The needs of a parent, receiving information about their child's performance in National Curriculum tests, are different from those of a Headteacher reviewing the performance of groups of pupils in their school. Their needs differ from the needs of central government monitoring performance over a period of years. The needs of test development agencies monitoring the effectiveness of their tests are different again. In each of these cases, the user should (although rarely does) have some feel for the reliability of the information on which they are making their judgements. Not only should they have some feel for the reliability of the information, but they may be interested in very different dimensions of reliability. Reliability is a function of the tests themselves and the performance of those tested. The interest of users will lie somewhere on the continuum between the technical reliability (in the classical sense) of the tests themselves and the generalisability of test performance data for individual pupils and larger groupings.

Alastair Pollitt's paper on measuring and evaluating reliability in National Curriculum Assessment is an important contribution, not least because it challenges some of the orthodoxies of reliability measurement ('The concept of test reliability has outlived its usefulness. Its traditional formulation is misleading, inappropriate and inadequate for modern assessment.'), but also because it begins to explore the needs of different users of test information. The need to reconceptualise validity, dependability and reliability is explored well in Dylan Wiliam's paper of the same name.

The time has arrived when it is important for all involved in National Curriculum Assessment to stand back for a moment, to identify more clearly the needs of all users of performance data and to develop a **package** of evaluative measures encompassing those needs. It is likely that the package will include some measures which bear a close resemblance to those developed in the context of classical test theory; others will be innovative and more closely matched to the needs of criterion- and domain-referenced assessment. Some measures are likely to be based on qualitative judgements relating more closely, for example, to face validity and 'customer satisfaction'. The unhealthy dichotomy between quantitative and qualitative methodologies should not persist. The Evaluation and Monitoring Unit within the School Examinations and Assessment Council began work on identifying the contents of such a package. This work should be carried forward. The BERA could play an important role in identifying the needs of different users and coordinating the work of those involved in the field.

The interpretation and use of performance data will be greatly enhanced when such data are automatically accompanied by a package of evaluative measures designed to meet the interpretation needs of the full range of potential users.

Tom Christie, Centre for Formative Assessment Studies,
School of Education, University of Manchester

Papers by Pollitt, Schagen and Hutchison and Wiliam

At last, we have an emerging theory of achievement testing. For too long achievement testing has relied almost entirely on the technology of ability testing for its theory and its associated quality standards. The papers in this book begin to map out the specific issues associated with the analysis of tests which attempt to measure a defined and delimited achievement construct. The move to a defined domain changes the definition of validity, but in the current state of the National Curriculum in England and Wales the structures of subject domains are themselves no more than hypotheses so the validity issue is not thereby rendered less problematic. Within such a domain, adequately represented, unreliability becomes a human attribute, rather than an inherent characteristic of the testing instrument. There is much of additional value to be gained from the study of unexpected, i.e. unreliable response patterns and even more from the study of bias, repeatedly observed aberrations associated with the interaction of particular testee attributes with specific test segments. That study, in its infancy because the testing technology that makes it possible is only now being developed, raises the third central issue of utility. Why test and what are the educational consequences of making false educational decisions based on test outcomes?

In commenting on the chapters, I shall treat of each of these three issues in turn, validity as construct representation, unreliability as individual departures from the expected structure and utility in relation to educational decision-making, the essence of formative assessment.

Validity as construct representation

In discussing the validity of cognitive tests Embretson (1983) makes a valuable distinction between construct representation, the extent to which the nature of the thing measured is made manifest in the test itself, and nomothetic span, the extent to which the test discriminates between individual respondents in terms of their possession of the thing measured. She recognises content and face validity on the one hand as belonging to a quite distinct category from concurrent and predictive validity on the other. To lump them both together under a generic title is in effect a category error.

One of the aims of teaching in the context of universal compulsory education must surely be that everyone should achieve and all should have prizes, the credo of the mastery learning movement which gave an enormous boost to the development of criterion-referenced testing (cf. Bloom *et al.*, 1971). It follows that nomothetic span is an index of the failure of universal compulsory education and in some schools at least major teacher efforts will be directed to nullifying its effect. If one accepts this point of view then for achievement tests accurate construct representation is all, and the extent of nomothetic span is an empirical descriptor of the success of the education system, not a basis for evaluating the success of the test itself. In this way, aptitude and achievement tests can be seen as quite distinct. Aptitude tests have the opposite objective of maximising nomothetic span and in meeting that objective leave the nature of the underlying attribute, Cronbach's construct validity, as the object of empirical investigation outside the test itself.

On this analysis, which takes validity back to the earliest of Wiliam's categories, 'a property of an assessment (content validity)', the achievement test constructor's task has never been easier. The National Curriculum ten-Level scale defines each subject domain in a highly articulated way, with each Level associated with statements of attainment which have at least the implicit status of criteria. There has been much public debate about whether teachers should effectively tick off each SoA in turn, or take the group of SoAs as a kind of grade descriptor in assigning pupils to Levels. Test constructors too face this aggregation issue, which is likely to be resolved in such a way as to maximise Wiliam's reliability, 'the extent to which inferences about the parts of the domain *actually* assessed are warranted'. The criterial attribute of a National Curriculum Assessment is that an ordinal relation between scale Levels should be engineered through task selection and mark scheme construction.

Staying with Wiliam's useful hierarchical schema, to go beyond reliability to dependability, 'the extent to which inferences within the domain of assessment are warranted', is in my view premature. The most obvious inference, made explicit by Hutchison, is that a child at a Level can meet the requirements of all prior Levels. The extent to which that inference is supportable goes far beyond the responsibility of the test constructor since it depends equally on the intentions of the curriculum constructor and the strategies of teachers. In a field of knowledge like National Curriculum geography, there is a sequence of Levels but very few contingencies between Levels. The basis of this inference is not built into the curriculum. The extent to which the inference holds good will simply depend on the sequence in which teachers choose to cover the curriculum. If they teach Level 3 before Level 4 then the chances are that the child at Level 4 will recognise Level 3 material; otherwise there are no guarantees.

So far I have adopted a minimalist position within Wiliam's hierarchies in the interests of isolating the distinguishing features of achievement tests and deriving a basis for their evaluation, which I take to be reliable domain representation. Schagen equates reliability with reproducibility, but in achievement testing what should be demonstrably stable? Certainly not the achievement of testees, which we can assume to be an unstable attribute, either consolidating into new patterns if direct instruction has ceased or continuing to grow if the subject is still under active study. An emphasis on construct representation suggests that the acid test of reproducibility is that the same pattern of response can be observed in the test behaviour of any child. Such stability is won at the cost of a marked reduction in nomothetic span. As Wiliam implies, in low stakes achievement testing scores have much meaning (construct representation) and little significance (nomothetic span).

That emphasis is difficult for teachers to accept, witness the first reaction to standard assessment tasks of Key Stage 1 teachers, who felt that they had been told very little about the individual child. They had been conditioned as we all are by their experience of public examinations and were looking to a consequential basis of result use (Wiliam's Figure 1). However, public examinations are only ostensibly achievement tests. Their validity depends on the extent to which they support traditional interpretations and uses of results as measures of aptitude for further learning. That public examinations have evolved to serve the selection function accounts in large measure for our historical complacency with ability testing technology as the model of achievement test analysis. Perhaps only in final examiners' meetings for degree awards and in the borderline review procedures of some GCSE and A-level boards has construct representation played a key role in decision making. It is common in these circumstances to consider the pattern of performance and award different grades to candidates with the same total score. However, in the absence of a supporting rationale, this has always been seen by the participants as a somewhat dubious activity only to be undertaken with much agonising behind closed doors.

End of key stage assessments do not lead to selection decisions; our work in CFAS does however suggest that with the right support they can lead teachers to a re-evaluation of the effectiveness of educational treatments. In these circumstances, decisions to leave well alone and not modify the treatment for the succeeding class are predicated on the assumption that the same pattern of response will be observed in the new group of children. Thus teachers have stability across children as a working assumption about test results which are designed to help them plan for educational improvement. If a test is to be used for formative purposes, nomothetic span is a minor consideration compared to construct representation, reproducibility of the structure of the subject with different items and different children.

Reliability as conformity to an expected pattern

Reliability considerations have long been identified as one tool which test constructors can use in trying to establish construct representation, but the National Curriculum allows a range of levels of aggregation. Pollitt makes an argument for generalisabilty theory (Cronbach *et al.*, 1972) as the model of analysis, and certainly it deals with successive aggregates of different facets, e.g. attainment targets, in the same analysis. Its outcome is an index of the sufficiency of data to support inferences and a means of calculating how much similar data would be required for any desired degree of accuracy in the inferences. Unfortunately it is generally *post-hoc* in spite of its formative applications.

Schagen and Hutchison are using a much more powerful tool in Item Response Theory, which also disaggregates pupil and item variance (construct representation and nomothetic span), but in advance of use, an important consideration in National Curriculum test construction. In the context of the validity discussion, Schagen's decision to treat the item as fixed and the pupil as variable may prove to be an important step forward in the analysis of achievement tests. A comparable rethink will be required in the interpretation of such analyses.

Schagen appears to equate borderline children with unreliable children: in his simulation we have ideal pupils whose item variance is essentially a function of closeness to the borderline. But this is tautologous. A borderline child is recognisable as one who responds correctly to only a subset of the items which define a Level. Children above the borderline and children below the borderline should generate no variance. Schagen's sine curves are a set of superimposed unimodal curves with different central tendencies. It is a graphic representation of FM Lord's dictum that any cognitive test will be perfectly reliable if it is presented to a set of respondents who are either quite incapable of tackling it or are so much in advance of the test that it presents no challenges. Pupils who get every item correct or every item wrong generate no item by person variance; the only source of 'error' in the internal consistency coefficient which is the real focus of Pollitt's attack on classical reliability theory.

This is in no way to minimise the importance of these graphical results. Schagen has been able to demonstrate with independent item sets and independent pupil sets and under a variety of model assumptions that Levels 2 and 3 of AT3 in the mathematics National Curriculum are in urgent need of redefinition. The hypothesis of two years of normal educational progress between these Levels is comprehensively refuted. These are formative data for curriculum designers.

As to the cogency of the model, there is little to choose between the outcomes of the various simulations. It does not seem to make much difference if uncertainty is associated with pupils or with items, provided uncertainty is built into the model. What would be interesting to see is how Schagen's model will identify ill-fitting respondents, those who both succeed and fail at several Levels at once. Such identification is a standard feature of conventional IRT. Study of the distribution of ill-fitting children within and between schools promises to be an important way into accountability in terms of curriculum delivery. In one study we have completed in CFAS, ill-fitting children were found to be few and far-between in Northern Ireland science at Levels 4, 5 and 6. Fewer than 1 in 40 did not conform to expectation.

The pattern of expectation in the National Curriculum is well-defined and can be empirically demonstrated to apply in practice. Hutchison turns the pattern into an assumption. His Procrustean imputation is the strong Guttman assumption that Levels are not simply temporally prior one to the other. Examples of successful Guttman scales are few and far between though it is well-established that any scale with very large intervals will act like a Guttman scale, even though it lacks its deterministic properties (cf. Van der Ven, 1980), This phenomenon weighed heavily in the Task Group on Assessment and Testing's choice of two years of normal educational progress as the scale unit for National Curriculum Assessment. It was recognised that any finer grain analysis would call for detailed knowledge about educational progressions which simply was not available at the time. In this sense Hutchison is on safe ground, but it is difficult to see how the reliability of adaptive testing can be measured if it is assumed that the construct representation of the test is perfect.

It would have been interesting to know the result of computing his IRT solutions with missing data rather than assumed perfect fit to the expected pattern. Any decent IRT software has this facility. The problem with IRT is that although it produces person-free item statistics, the solutions are very sensitive to the other items present in the analysis. We have found in our work in CFAS that to make the Procrustean imputation stabilises solutions because so much goodness of fit is introduced into the analysis. Recognising missing data as such can lead to highly unstable outcomes, though admittedly on samples of only around 600 candidate responses. *Pace* Thissen (1993), we attribute the instability to the paucity of other items against which the item can be calibrated when there are relatively empty matrices.

It is this paucity of items which is in greatest need of investigation. IRT makes a strong unidimensionality assumption. The National Curriculum and indeed all achievement domains are highly differentiated. Unidimensionality is only a local feature. We must await the outcome of attempts (cf. Haertel, 1990) to reconcile the multiple facets characteristic of generalisability theory with IRT before we can be sure that out test construction technology is in accord with our emerging test theory.

Utility as the basis of educational decisions

The arguments for a revised view of both validity and reliability derive from the criterion-referenced nature of educational achievement tests. Criterion-referencing allows structured tests which carry maximum feedback to the teacher in making decisions about educational treatments. But criterion-referencing carried a penalty in individual decision making.

In traditional norm-referenced tests, standards are expressed as summations, say 50 per cent success for a pass. In such a system opposite errors, false positives and false negatives, tend to cancel each other out with the result that error as a proportion of the whole diminishes as the number of elements summed increases. In a criterion-referenced test, aggregation is combinatorial. Success is defined as the demonstration of attribute i AND attribute ii AND (attribute iii OR attribute iv). The greater the number of ANDs, the lower the passing percentage. This is simple probability. If a Level is defined by one criterion, a probability of .5 on the criterion gives a probability of .5 of attaining the Level. However, to have a probability of .5 of attaining a Level defined by two criteria, the candidate needs a probability of just over .7 of attaining each criterion (for such a candidate the assumption of local independence holds (Lazarsfeld, 1950)), and for a three-criterion Level the probability of attaining each of the separate criteria must be just under .8, falling back to .5 if only two of the three criteria (the 'n-1' rule) are required. This is not strictly speaking bias (see Hutchison Chapter 7), since it applies to all respondents equally, but it does present test constructors with real problems of content representation. Where a two-criteria Level succeeds an 'any two from three' Level, efforts to make the tasks at the upper Level suitably accessible tend to blur the distinction in attainment required by the tasks at the two Levels. If preserving exemplification of the distinction in attainment in each separate task is given primacy, and an 'any two from three criteria' Level succeeds a two-criteria Level, then the distinction of candidate Level performance gets blurred, precisely the outcome in Schagen's Ma3 data.

Which of these risks we should run depends on the costs and benefits of false positive and false negative decisions. Novick and Jackson (1974) deal with this issue by means of the Regret Ratio, an elaboration of the signal detection theory which Wiliam rightly draws to our attention as an important analytic tool. The Regret Ratio estimates the relative seriousness of false positives and false negatives against four sources of regret: statistical error, content error, student motivation and societal cost. In selection decisions, false positives through statistical (nomothetic) error carry a high social cost. In decisions to progress, false negatives through content (representation) error carry a high cost in student motivation.

Our current progression rules are neutral with respect to progression decisions for the genuinely borderline candidate in only two instances: single-criterion Levels and Levels with three statements of attainment where the 'n-1' rule is in force. In all other attainment target Levels, the true borderline candidate is at least three times more likely not to be awarded the Level as to be progressed to the next Level. Whether that is a satisfactory state of affairs we have not the slightest idea because our conventional approaches to test analysis have not made the matter manifest for subsequent educational evaluation. Thus while I remain firmly of the opinion that the prime responsibility of the test constructor is construct representation, I have to agree with Wiliam that it is only when our practice can take full account of the educational decisions likely to be based on the tests that achievement test theory will have come of age.

Conclusion

Pragmatic and *post hoc* estimation of distributions (Pollitt) is a task we face if we are to model the system (Schagen) successfully. How internally coherent is the model itself? How reliable are children in terms of consistency with the National Curriculum model (Hutchison)? How successful are construct representative tests in informing teachers' decisions (Wiliam)? These are key questions with profound educational implications. They have been raised by the contributors in a variety of ways, each seeking an appropriate technology of educational achievement testing. A new theoretical stance is beginning to emerge. It now itself needs to be put to the test of close and continuing scrutiny of the rich national database which is under construction.

References

BLOOM, A.G., HASTINGS, J.T. and MADAUS, G.F. (1971). *Handbook On Formative and Summative Evaluation of Student Learning*, New York: McGraw-Hill.

CRONBACH, L.J., GLASER, G.C., NANDA, H. and RAJARATNAM, N. (1972). *The Dependability of Behavioural Measurements: Theory of Generalizability for Scores and Profiles*, New York:, Wiley.

EMBRETSON, S.E. (1983). 'Construct validity: Construct representation versus nomothetic span', *Psychological Bulletin*, **83**, .178-87.

HAERTEL, E.H. (1990). 'Continuous and discrete latent structure models for item response data', *Psychometrika*, **66**, 477-94.

LAZARSFELD, P.F. (1950). The logical and mathematical foundation of latent structure analysis. In: STOUFFER, S.A., GUTTMAN, L., SUCHMAN, E.A., LAZARSFELD, P.F. STAR, S.A. and CLAUSEN, J.A. (Eds.) *Studies in Social Psychology in World War II, Vol. 4: Measurement and Prediction*, 362-412. Princeton, NJ: Princeton University Press.

NOVICK, M.R. and JACKSON, P.H. (1974). *Statistical Methods for Educational and Psychological Research*, New York, McGraw-Hill.

THISSEN, D. (1993) Repealing rules that no longer apply to psychological measurement. In FREDERIKSON, N., MISLEVY, R.J. and BEJAR, I.I. (Eds.) *Test heory for a New Generation of Tests*. Hilladale, NJ:, Lawrence Erlbaum Associates.

Van der VEN, A. H. (1980). *Introduction to Scaling*. New York: Wiley Interscience.